The Bare-Knuckle Boxer's Companion

THE BARE-KNUCKLE BOXER'S COMPANION

Learning How to Hit Hard and Train Tough from the Early Boxing Masters

DAVID LINDHOLM AND ULF KARLSSON

PALADIN PRESS • BOULDER, COLORADO

Also by David Lindholm:
Sigmund Ringeck's Knightly Art of the Longsword (with Peter Svärd)
Sigmund Ringeck's Knightly Arts of Combat: Sword and Buckler Fighting, Wrestling, and Fighting in Armor (with Peter Svärd)
Masters of Medieval and Renaissance Martial Arts: Rediscovering the Western Combat Heritage (contributor)

*The Bare-Knuckle Boxer's Companion: Learning How to Hit Hard
  and Train Tough from the Early Boxing Masters*
by David Lindholm and Ulf Karlsson Tada

ISBN 13: 978-1-58160-700-0
Printed in the United States of America

Published by Paladin Press, a division of
Paladin Enterprises, Inc.
Gunbarrel Tech Center
7077 Winchester Circle
Boulder, Colorado 80301 USA
+1.303.443.7250

Direct inquiries and/or orders to the above address.

Visit our website at www.paladin-press.com

WARNING

Some of the techniques depicted in this book are dangerous. It is not the intent of the authors or publisher to encourage readers to attempt any of them without proper professional supervision and training. Attempting to do so can result in severe injury or death. Do not attempt any of these techniques or drills without the supervision of a qualified instructor.

The authors, publisher, and distributors of this book disclaim any liability from any damage or injury of any type that a reader or user of information contained in this book may incur from the use or misuse of said information. This book is *for academic study only*.

CONTENTS

INTRODUCTION

This book deals with the European art of fighting by using the hands for striking—the martial art of pugilism, or bare-knuckle boxing. We are not talking about the modern *sport* of boxing. We are going to deal with something else here; namely how to fight using your hands without gloves, wraps, and other aids. The modern sport of boxing is a tough and valuable practice that certainly has self-defense applications, but it is an athletic contest, which means it is regulated and relatively safe. Bare-knuckle boxing, on the other hand, is historically speaking a martial art, at least in the modern sense, as well as a sport. It involves slightly different techniques, methods of training, and even perhaps another sort of fighter—similar to the modern boxer, yet not identical.

Our book is intended as a how-to guide, a companion of sorts, rather than a discourse on the history of bare-knuckle boxing. We've included some aspects of history, because it is important to understand the context of one's field of study. But our main focus is to extract the practical material from historical bare-knuckle boxing and show how it can be applied in modern self-defense.

Exceptionally skilled people who fight with bare hands still exist today. I am thinking of the Irish and the Gypsies, who stand out as the last proponents of the old bare-knuckle art. If you have a chance, seek them out and learn from them and assimilate what is good. Learn what you can from the old masters we deal with in this book, as well from such great boxers as Sullivan, Dempsey, Marciano, and Ali. Fighting unarmed with the hands is a simple concept but a complex skill, too complex to be encompassed by one book, person, or martial art system. Therefore, learn from as many relevant sources as possible.

Don't be fooled by the seemingly quaint, antiquated poses of the boxers in the period illustrations. The fighters of the bare-knuckle era were tough men and skilled combatants. They had to be in order to endure brutal, often bloody bouts that could last for hours. To demonstrate their techniques as clearly as possible, we have adapted their somewhat formal postures. When actually applying bare knuckle in a self-defense situation or during a training session, the action would be much more dynamic.

Please remember that a person who trains in bare-knuckle boxing is training to be a hard hitter. Therefore, be responsible with what you do with this knowledge, whether in training or in a real confrontation.

WHO ARE WE?

My name is David Lindholm, and I have an MA in history and medieval archaeology, amongst a whole lot of other degrees, from Lund University in Sweden (and other places, come to think of it). I have been practicing martial arts since 1977, when my father took me to a wrestling club. I have trained in karate, boxing, sport fencing, iaido, kendo, wrestling, and tai chi chuan, but since 1996 my main fields have been historical European martial arts and Japanese *koryu* sword arts. I have written on the medieval long sword, sword and buckler, medieval wrestling, and the quarterstaff.

My interest in the early European martial arts led me to consider the art of pugilism. During my university studies, I had come across illustrations of Greek and Roman pugilists that piqued my curiosity. Later, I discovered material on post-medieval bare-knuckle boxing in libraries and archives. This book is a result of that curiosity and the subsequent work—and lots of sweat—that went into my hands-on study of bare-knuckle boxing.

Ulf Karlsson studied business administration and Japanese at Växjö University and later took part in the Programme for East and South East Asian Studies (with a focus on Japan) at Lund University, including an exchange year at Waseda University. He started training in Taido—a Japanese martial art created by Okinawan Seiken Shukumine—in 1984 and has instructed in that art since 1987, currently holding the grade of Godan Renshi. Since 1992, Ulf has visited Japan more than 10 times to train, usually staying for three months per visit. He was a member of the Swedish Taido team from 1991–1999 and was the ladies' national team coach from 2003–2005. He has taught Taido in several countries, including Denmark, Finland, Netherlands, and Japan. Currently, Ulf is exploring the classical kata of the teacher Soko Kishimoto as a way to better understand the roots of Taido. Ulf has also trained in ESDS (Explosive Self Defence System) with Slavo Godzik, Splashing Hands with James McNeil, Ryu Te with Robert Rousselot, and most recently the Okinawan martial art Te with Mark Bishop.

Remember, this is our own interpretation of the sources; as such, it is bound to include our own misunderstandings and preconceptions. Therefore, be critical and always return to the original sources. Please also remember that still pictures will always, to some extent, fail to capture the movement and dynamics of all martial arts. The techniques should be understood as changing, dynamic, and expressive rather than static.

1

THE PUGILISTIC ARTS IN EUROPE

Our aim for this chapter is not to write an in-depth history of the art of pugilism. Other more learned scholars can and have done that. Instead, we will sketch a brief history that serves as a backdrop to the actual techniques and advice on how to fight that follow in the technique chapters.

We have to go far back to find the first sources of an unarmed system of combat—i.e., striking with the hands, with some kicking, a few throws, and an elbow for good measure—practiced in Europe. The first traces emerged in ancient Greece and Rome, which we will discuss in more detail below. But first, it is significant to note that the style of boxing practiced in Greece and Rome corresponds closely with the system as it survived on the British Isles. We would even go so far as to hypothesize that bare-knuckle boxing is the direct descendant of the ancient art of pugilism as seen in Greek and Roman boxing. In other parts of the world, fighting systems using the hands came up with different ideas and solutions, but we believe that the close resemblance of British pugilism to the evidence we see in ancient art is not a coincidence.

From Greece to Spain to North Africa, we can find traces of the same pugilistic system, but not in the far-flung regions of the empire, in Persia and India or in the outlying Germanic areas. The core areas seem to be the European heart of the ancient Roman world, and in some respects Britain was one of the most Romanized areas of the entire empire. This seemingly unbroken line is remarkable, since it opens up the possibility of a surviving system of unarmed combat that is both the oldest still practiced today as well as a true Western unarmed martial heritage stretching back to the learning of classical Greece and the glory of ancient Roman.

So let us begin this little trip back in time and see what the evidence has to say and, along the way, pick up the foundations of the art of bare-knuckle boxing.

BOXING IN ANCIENT GREECE

We must go back to ancient Greece to find the first recorded traces of unarmed arts on the European continent. No doubt such arts were practiced in other parts of Europe, but no evidence of them has been uncovered. In Greece, however, the unarmed arts—in the form of wrestling and in the legendary art of pankration, sadly lost to us—were not only a method of personal combat; they were an integral part of a young man's education. Pankration and wrestling were part of the Pythian and Panathenaic Games, two of the recurring sports festivals of ancient Greece (one of which was resurrected as the modern Olympic Games). Frequently, participants in pankration contests died or sustained injuries that crippled them for life. (Pankration is worth noting because it contained both wrestling and striking techniques, which is what we are looking for in a modern martial art suitable for self-defense. The art of wrestling we leave aside for others to deal with.)

Black-figure depiction of the Pananthenaic games showing either a pankration or boxing match. Notice the attempted chancery along with the strike, as well as the attempt to block the attack by the fighter being held.

From the island of present-day Santorini (ancient Thera), we have the oldest illustration of pugilism in the world. It is a wall painting of two adolescents boxing, wearing gloves on their right hands. The style is influenced by the Minoan civilization of Crete, and dating sets it at about 1500 B.C. [1]

We also find boxing, or fighting with the hands, mentioned in Homer's *Iliad* (dating uncertain, but let's say around 1000 B.C.), where the use of *himantes* is mentioned. These thongs of leather, the precursors of the rather vicious Roman *caestus* (or *cestus*), protected the hands by wrapping around as much as boxing wraps do today. (For a superb look at *himantes*, see the wraps in detail on the bronze statue from the 1st century B.C. shown below.[2])

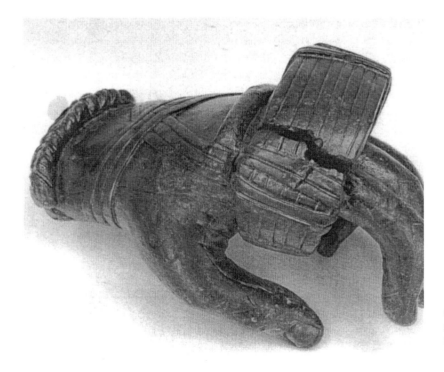

Close-up of the 1st century B.C. bronze piece showing the wrappings of the boxer's hand and the *himantes* tied in place over the knuckles.

The *Iliad* passage is the first *recorded* account of pugilism in the Western world and is well worth reading as a whole.

So spake he, and forthwith uprose a man valiant and tall, [665] well-skilled in boxing, even Epeius, son of Panopeus; and he laid hold of the sturdy mule, and spake, saying: Let him draw nigh, whoso is to bear as his prize the two-handled cup: the mule I deem that none other of the Achaeans shall lead away, by worsting me with his fists, for I avow me to be the best man. [670] Sufficeth it not that I fall short in battle? One may not, meseemeth, prove him a man of skill in every work. For thus will I speak, and verily this thing shall be brought to pass: utterly will I rend his flesh and crush his bones. Wherefore let them that be next of kin abide here in a throng, [675] that they may bear him forth when worsted by my hands. So spake he, and they all became hushed in silence. Euralyus alone uprose to face him, a godlike man, son of king Mecisteus, son of Talaus, who on a time had come to Thebes for the burial of Oedipus, [680] when he had fallen, and there had worsted all the sons of Cadmus. And Tydeus son, famed for his spear, made Euryalus ready, heartening him with words, and much he wished for him victory. A girdle first he cast about him, and thereafter gave him well-cut thongs of the hide of an ox of the field. [685] So the twain, when they had girded themselves, stepped into the midst of the place of gathering, and lifting their mighty hands on high one against the other, fell to, and their hands clashed together in heavy blows. Dread then was the grinding of their teeth, and the sweat flowed on every side from off their limbs. But upon him goodly Epeius rushed [690] as he peered for an opening, and smote him on the cheek, nor after that, methinks, did he long stand upright, for

Greek piece with two boxers trading punches, straight strikes by the look of it. Notice the closeness of their leading feet and the wrappings on both hands.

even there did his glorious limbs sink beneath him. And as when beneath the ripple of the North Wind a fish leapeth up on the tangle-strewn sand of a shallow, and then the black wave hideth it, even so leapt up Euryalus when he was smitten. But great-souled Epeius [695] took him in his hands and set him on his feet, and his dear comrades thronged about him and led him through the place of gathering with trailing feet, spitting out clotted blood and letting his head hang to one side; and they brought him wandering in his wits and set him down in the midst of their company, and themselves went and fetched the two-handled cup. [3]

In Greek art, the boxer was portrayed less frequently than the wrestler, who seems to have represented a much more common form of personal unarmed combat and physical regimen. There is an interesting piece of evidence as to why this may have been the case, and it is found in the words of the philosopher Socrates, as told to us by his student Plato. The philosopher makes two roundabout references to boxers, the first from the dialog *Gorgias*:

> [515e] . . . on the assumption that he was a good citizen.
>
> **Callicles:** Well, what then?
>
> **Socrates:** Nothing: but tell me one thing in addition—whether the Athenians are said to have become better because of Pericles, or quite the contrary, to have been corrupted by him. What I, for my part, hear is that Pericles has made the Athenians idle, cowardly, talkative, and avaricious, by starting the system of public fees.
>
> **Callicles:** You hear that from the folk with battered ears, Socrates.
>
> **Socrates:** Ah, but what is no longer a matter of hearsay, but rather of certain knowledge, for you as well as for me, is that Pericles was popular at first, and the Athenians passed no degrading sentence upon him so long as they were "worse"; but as soon as they had been made upright and honorable by him . . . [4]

What is Plato talking about when he refers to people "with battered ears"? Generally, this is taken by classical scholars to be a reference to the Spartans, who seem to have been much more fond of boxing than the civilized Athenians, and if you box much you will get battered ears.

The second quote is along the same lines:

Greek black-figure amphora with two boxers, the left with a nose bleed. Notice the closeness of their leading feet and the wrappings on both hands. It is difficult to say who is striking or blocking, but it seems as if a hook has been executed.

ABOVE: Greek krater showing two boxers on the left. The combatant on the right is striking and the one on the left is blocking the attack.

RIGHT: Greek boxer. Notice the coverings on both hands, indicating that he strikes with both, and the extended guard, with the other hand coiled back to strike.

[342b] . . . and sophists are more numerous in those regions: but the people there deny it and make pretence of ignorance, in order to prevent the discovery that it is by wisdom that they have ascendancy over the rest of the Greeks, like those sophists of whom Protagoras was speaking; they prefer it to be thought that they owe their superiority to fighting and valor, conceiving that the revelation of its real cause would lead everyone to practice this wisdom. So well have they kept their secret that they have deceived the followers of the Spartan cult in our cities, with the result that some get broken ears . . . [5]

Plato here refers to people who were sympathetic to the Spartan way of life, one that emphasized the arts of combat in all their forms. Unfortunately, Sparta was not known for its fine artisans and exquisite prose, and thus we have scant evidence of boxing from that culture. However, boxing was evidently seen as being enough of a characteristic of the Spartans for Socrates to make a joke about it, giving it at least some credibility as a piece of circumstantial evidence.

Physical evidence of pugilism from classical Greece exists mainly in the form of paintings and decorations on ceramics and statues. A society like Sparta, with limited emphasis on producing art, would have left fewer pieces of evidence for us to find, but fortunately we have other examples. We see, for instance, two boxers in an Attic black-figure amphora painted by Antimedes of Rhodes, one throwing a straight punch to the opponent's stomach. [6] On another Attic black figure Samos from the 6th century B.C., we see two boxers in a fight, one throwing a straight punch. Curiously, both wear loincloths. This was not common among the Greeks, who preferred to exercise in the nude, but it was common among the Etrurians on the Italian peninsula. This leads one to wonder if boxing was also enjoyed there, [7] especially since this particular item is considered to have been made for export to Etruria, which means the decoration would have had to been one that was sellable there. Boxing was obviously taken to have been such an appealing decoration.

Greek amphora Attic black figure Samos of two boxers, 6th century B.C. The left figure is striking from below. Notice how close they stand as well as the bent arms, indicating close-in work and thus no reliance on long, straight strikes only.

Attic black-figure amphora by Antimedes of Rhodes, depicting two boxers. Again, notice the closeness and the even guard of the left fighter, who is possibly beating down the opponent's left arm to create an opening. Alternatively, it may show the fighter on the right striking at the opponent's stomach.

BOXING IN ANCIENT ROME

In the Roman world, boxing became more popular than wrestling for an obvious reason—while the Greeks *practiced* wrestling and sports mainly for health and competition, the Romans enjoyed *looking* at other people doing it. And to be frank, wrestling is not that exciting to watch, whereas two grown men pummelling each other into the ground has an undeniable entertainment value, as we recognize even today.

Boxing in the Roman world was at first a minor event at the games, overshadowed by chariot racing and gladiator sports. But boxing became more popular as time went on, and as it became more popular, the bloodiness of the bouts increased. If we look at the rather limited evidence of boxing in the Roman world, we see this rise of its "blood sport" aspect, such as the *himantes* of the Greeks evolving into the bronze or copper *caestus* of the Roman arena. This is not to say that Greek boxing was not hard on the practitioner, but the Romans often made a point of staging things so that it would be more of a bloody spectacle to entertain the crowd.

While we have at least circumstantial evidence

Two boxers from the Roman Empire, 1st–2nd century B.C.

that boxing or pugilism was practiced in ancient Greece as a martial art (at least by the Spartans, the most martial of all the Greek city states), we have no such evidence from the Roman era. A simple explanation might well be that wrestling was emphasized more because of its potential practical application on the battlefield. It is not that practical to punch a man in armour and helmet on the battlefield, but you can wrestle him down and finish him there. Boxing in the ancient world, therefore, would not have been as important as wrestling from a purely martial perspective. And this perspective seems to have carried over into the medieval world.

BOXING IN THE MEDIEVAL WORLD

In our quest to trace the roots of pugilism, we found that the medieval world has left us the greatest treasures in the form of manuals of personal combat. Yet for reasons that are unclear, the evidence from these manu-

Jack Broughton (left) and his opponent, George Stevenson, depicted in a suitably muscular pose at George Taylor's gymnasium in February 1741.

als suggests that medieval unarmed combat focused on wrestling rather than striking and kicking. The assertion that it was due to the inefficiency of striking a man in armour ignores the fact that, in most areas of medieval life, men fought men without armour (e.g., common brawls). Whereas the ancient world emphasized wrestling in unarmed combat, the evidence suggests that boxing and wrestling were practiced side-by-side and coexisted as two coherent systems. The medieval world seems to have neglected the striking arts.

But if we look closer at the unarmed combat manuals of the 15th century, we find strikes—perhaps not presented as a coherent system, but sprinkled here and there among the wrestling techniques. This is seen in the works of Sigmund Ringeck, Johann Paschen, and others. (More on this in chapter 6.)

One of the most prominent of all medieval masters, Fiore dei Liberi, actually mentions boxers or pugilists in the foreword of his magnum opus from 1409, *Flos Duellatorum Dimicandi*, where he says, "I have decided to compose a book with regard to the things most useful in this splendid art, placing in it several figures and with examples of those methods of attack and defense and parries which the astuteness of the squire or the boxer can themselves be served" (*Fiore dei Liberi Pissano Dossi Ms*, translation by the Exiles). What is inter-

Bare-knuckle fight in the 19th century. Notice the guard positions and the close distance between the fighters.

esting is that, while Master Fiore does not seem to have been a boxer himself, he mentions them as an example of astute people in the introduction to his major work. They therefore must have been recognized as being representatives of that description in Italy at that time, or his wording would have been pointless. Circumstantial evidence, but it is there.

Master Fiore's work is representative of medieval combat manuals in that it includes a detailed, solid section on wrestling but not one on boxing. However, most wrestling texts of the medieval (and post-medieval) world contained strikes and kicks, indicating a multi-technique system. Wrestling moves dominate, but this emphasis was probably due to the fact that wrestling was both a combat art and a form of entertainment. Wrestling matches were a staple of the jester groups travelling the lands, as a common spectacle at fairs, or just as a simple pastime.

But there may have been more prosaic reasons for this emphasis. Wrestling allows for a degree of control that pugilism does not. Boxing as recreation does not work well because it requires aggression, whereas wrestling allows for an easier approach. Wrestling matches can certainly become aggressive, but it is easier to maintain control and safety. If you learn to strike with your bare hands with a modicum of technique, you can damage your opponent severely. This is not something that a travelling group could afford to do, let alone friends enjoying a little friendly competition after work. Add to that the fact that it is hard to strike a man in armour and we have a good idea why wrestling moves dominated in the medieval martial texts.

BOXING IN THE POST-MEDIEVAL WORLD

Interest in the pugilistic arts seems to have taken off in earnest in the 18th century, when we begin to see an increasing number of texts dealing with pugilism, as well as reports of matches and masters of the art. It is from this tradition, especially from the British Isles, that we get the bulk of our material on bare-knuckle boxing today. This includes the work of such bare-knuckle greats as Daniel Mendoza (*The Art of Boxing*, 1789), Thomas Fewtrell (*Boxing Reviewed*, 1790), Edmund Price (*The Science of Self Defence*, 1867), and James Sullivan (*Boxing*, 1893).

This rise of pugilism corresponds roughly with the decrease of other forms of combative sports, i.e., martial arts played for fun, with some general agreements to reduce injuries. In England and Germany, these events still could be rather bloody affairs, involving polearms and swords. By narrowing the focus to fistfights only and introducing other limitations, the pugilistic arts gradually evolved into the safer but still rough sport of bare knuckle.

Originally, there seems to have been very few restrictions in bare knuckle. Basically, you could not use weapons, kick a man lying down, or bite him. The bare-knuckle era ended in the early 20th century when gloves were introduced, stricter rules were instituted, and oversight organizations formed. These developments focused on enhancing the safety of the combatants, and this led to the loss of knowledge of striking without gloved hands, as well as such techniques as throws, kicks, and elbows. The remainder of this book is devoted to reviving this practical combative art.

NOTES

1. Doumas, *Santorini: A Guide to the Island and Its Archaeological Treasures*.
2. Pedly, *Greek Art and Archaeology*, p. 338.
3. Homer, *Iliad*.
4. Plato, *Gorgias*.
5. Plato, *Protagoras*.
6. Boardman, *The History of Greek Vases*, p. 161.
7. Boardman, *The History of Greek Vases*, pp. 236–237.

2

BARE-KNUCKLE BASIC TECHNIQUES

First, a preliminary note on our interpretation of the techniques. When working with this material, we were faced with several difficult issues. Sadly, many of the engravings available to us for interpretation are not that good. The artist often was not able to depict anatomy in a biomechanically correct manner—there are shortened legs; impossible angles in knees, elbows, and feet; stylized positions of the legs; and so on. Facing that, we preferred to let the illustrations take a back seat in favor of the descriptive text that the masters wrote, which is often clear, understandable, and accurate. We tested the biomechanical foundation of each technique, since this never changes regardless of the century and society in which one lives. The version of the technique at which we arrived was then applied in a fighting situation, where we tried to punch each other out. If it worked, we kept it; if not, we assumed we got it wrong and went back to the drawing board.

It is important not to simply do what a text says or copy an engraving. There are, for instance, many ways to throw your head and body back, as Mendoza advises, but how do we know which way he meant? To find a solution, we opted to solve the problem in the manner described above. It is not perfect, but there are limited ways in which we can bypass the veil of time and discover the veracity of the descriptions. All interpreters of martial arts, working without a living tradition, will struggle with this problem when developing their material. We therefore wish to emphasize that this is our understanding of these techniques at this time, and it will absolutely change over time.

At the same time, it is evident that the techniques described in the old texts were intended to be guidelines. As in all martial arts, duplicating a movement will not make you victorious by that action alone. On the contrary, the *principle* of the technique must be internalized by finding your own way of executing it. We are all different, so we need to find ways to make things work for each of us, first by copying as close as possible the original technique, then leaving the level of the child and striking out into an adult world of actually understanding what we do and making it our own. As long as you comply with biomechanical principles, the movement will be sound and work well.

In bare-knuckle boxing, this means to investigate the guards, strikes, and parries closely, to copy them as faithfully as possible, and, once that can be done with ease, to develop a variety that suit you personally. This is a scientific process of constantly testing your thesis in order to arrive at a new synthesis, to develop your boxing and not fall into the trap of stagnation by saying, "Now I am copying the illustrations, so now I know it all."

The bare-knuckle fight of today is surrounded by much mystique and plenty of thrills. We can purchase DVDs of illegal fights recorded with hand-held cameras, many of them originating from the British Isles. (For an amazing account of a modern-day bare-knuckle hero, read *King of the Gypsies*, the story of Bartly Gorman, undefeated bare-knuckle champion of England and Ireland.) These fights are illuminating in many respects. One of the most important points is that what is today labeled as bare-knuckle boxing has little or no resemblance to the system that was developed in ancient Greece and Rome. It has passed and changed through many hands until it came to rest in England's green and pleasant land. Parts of the ancient art remain, but not as a coherent system. What survives today often arrived from sport boxing.

Another important point is that bare-knuckle boxing is a European fighting art, developed for Europeans. It differs from many forms of Asian martial arts in that it was developed for our climate, constitution, and way of life. Thai boxing is very impressive, but face it: Ulf and I live in Sweden, and for six months of the year it is a bit hard to pull off a high kick or knee strike simply because of restrictive clothing or difficult ground. A reasonable conclusion would probably be that *all fighting arts develop in a context.* Taken out of that context, they lose much of their practical applicability.

It is important to preserve and nourish this European fighting art, especially since it is both easy to learn (but difficult to master, as are all arts) and effective to use. Bare-knuckle boxing was not boxing with the hands only, not even in the ring until fairly late. Although limitations were imposed because participants were severely injured or killed during bouts (a testament to the effectiveness of the art), such non-hand techniques as throws and locks are well documented. And these were the types of unpleasant techniques that did mechanical damage to the opponent rather than simply pin or immobilize him. The attitude seemed to be, "If you are doing a throw, why on earth land him on something other than the back of his head?"

Sport boxing works quite well as a self-defense art, especially if you make a few changes to it, as Ned Beaumont points out in his books (see chapter 9). It remains, however, a sport, because it requires gloves, a ring, timed rounds, and other limitations. Gloves alone allow you to punch less well and still have a functioning hand, and they guard you to some extent, in essence giving you a form of shield that is not there once the gloves come off. Remove the gloves and the sport paraphernalia and everything changes. That said, many boxers are more than able to adapt their art and make it effective for self-defense, and boxing is an unquestionably effective physical fitness regimen.

Bare-knuckle boxing is, however, what boxing was before it turned into today's modern spectator sport. We can say that most of the old bare-knuckle techniques are not that useful in the ring but are very much of use on the street. But you really cannot compare the bare-knuckle martial art with the sport of boxing; it is not fair to either art, and we therefore will not make any comparisons at all, except when we want to emphasize an important difference to explain an aspect of bare knuckle that might seem strange or out of place.

THE BASIC TECHNIQUES

The system—for a system it is—of bare-knuckle boxing is not a precisely fixed one. Depending on which master we consulted, and which point in time we chose to examine, we found slightly different techniques and tactics. Here it is important to make the distinction between those masters who taught a system for fighting primarily in a ring, such as Daniel Mendoza in his influential work, and, for instance, Edmund Price, who in his 1867 book, *The Science of Self Defence*, includes techniques such as simple wrestling moves and holds, which were not allowed in the ring in his time but which are essential to self-defense. Price's book shows also that the bare-knuckle art was not a sport only, as boxing historians wish us to believe—it was a fighting art, and as such it could be put to many different uses. A quote from Mr. Price:

> Our object, then, in this volume is to give a correct and reliable Manual on the "Art of Self Defence", not founded on "obsolete" rules of a by-gone age, but on the practical results of our own experience.

Price's manual is a useful introduction to bare knuckle simply because he is one of the last great exponents to write on the art as it was evolving into modern sport boxing, and he is very lucid and has included some excellent illustrations that enable us to unlock what he wants us to do. Price is also one of the few writers on the subject who deal with the art primarily from a self-defense perspective. Other writers mention that it might be good to know how to box if you are set upon by "footpads" in the city but do not go into self-defense as such. Given the words of Price and others, we can surmise that at least a few considered it to be a defensive art as well as a sporting activity. It is essential, however, to understand that the varying advice given by Price, Mendoza, Fewtrell, Allanson-Winn, and all the anonymous authors—even up to the influential work of Jack Dempsey, who gave advice on how to punch properly with ungloved hands based on knowledge from the bare-knuckle era—does not cancel each other out. You will see how they and many other masters give roughly similar advice, but the arena differs, and thus the techniques themselves differ.

In the following section, we will examine the basic techniques and advice of various masters. We have made an editorial decision to include only what we consider to be the more important points and techniques from several sources. In doing this, we had to exclude some material that we simply felt did not work after testing it.

The Guard Position

Let us begin with the basic guard position. It is similar to the modern boxer's stance, but there were different versions. Important in all of them was that the guard had to protect the head and the "mark" (the area around the solar plexus), while allowing for powerful strikes and agile foot movement. Mobility in particular is essential for good defense. Mendoza states that parrying is OK, but it is better to void the attack, and to do this effectively you must have mobility. This may be the reason why so many boxers of the bare-knuckle era fought somewhat upright compared to what we are used to seeing today. It was a narrower stance, offering greater mobility but at the cost of stability.

That said, how do we make sense of period illustrations showing widely spaced legs? It is significant to note

Guard positions in the fight, late 18th century. Note the widely spaced legs.

Boxer in a guard position. Again, note the wide stance.

that you find the same generic leg position in illustrations showing people engaging in activities as varied as boxing, dancing, plowing, fishing, and watching others do a whole host of different things. Later in the 19th century, when photos and more natural forms of printing images start to appear, we see these positions become more upright, with more closely spaced legs. In terms of boxing, there is a fundamental truth: wide-spaced legs mean hitting harder; narrow-spaced legs mean moving faster. These stances and their advantages are not interchangeable, unfortunately. But consider that moving and striking are not the same thing. This means you can have an upright, narrow stance when on guard and step out into a wide one to generate more power when striking.

Humphreys (right) and Mendoza (left) setting to. Notice the rather similar guard position and how their feet are overlapping, but they lean away with their upper bodies.

Guard positions of Humphreys on the left and Mendoza on the right, from a book by one of Mendoza's students.

Mendoza shows a stance where he leans slightly forward at the waist, but with the body upright. The feet are shoulder-width apart, but the lead foot is more to the side than the front, creating a more square stance. The legs have a pronounced bend in the knees, his weight is on the lead leg, and he is guarding his face with the hands positioned almost parallel in front of his chin, with the left slightly more forward. Mendoza's crouched posture withdraws his mark as far from his opponent as possible. This stance offers very good protection and will let you strike faster blows in more rapid succession compared to other guards. The downside is that you will not get your body behind your strikes to the same extent as you would with a more upright position.

Mendoza's stance should also be understood in light of the fact that several sources say he was a somewhat short man. If you are short, your reach will be shorter than many opponents. To counter this you must move in close, but as you do you risk getting hit. A possible solution is to make yourself even smaller while protecting your face with your hands so that when the opponent tries to strike you, he will at best hit the top of your head as he strikes downward. This works well whether you are short or simply prefer to crouch. Your reach will suffer, though, as will the ease with which you move since you must by necessity bend your knees more and widen the stance. Although this will slow you down as you move, it does not mean you cannot move—just watch modern boxers who use this type of stance for proof of that. It does mean, however, that any change in your angular direction will be slower since your base is wider.

Mendoza in a guard position. Notice the equidistance of the hands.

Ulf demonstrating the basic
guard stance. (See illustration
at top left on page 16.)

Mendoza's crouched stance.

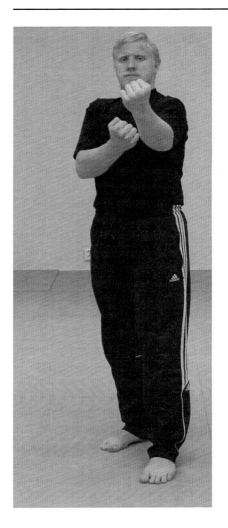

Ulf demonstrating Humphreys' rear stance.

Richard Humphreys (sometimes seen spelled as "Humphries" and other variations), who is the second figure in the copperplate found at the beginning of Mendoza's classic work, *The Art of Boxing*, is in a rear stance. This position is the one we are all familiar with from photographs of boxers from the 19th century. It is considered old and not that effective, but what is crucial to remember is that these men fought without gloves. Gloves may not seem like much, but they do make a difference—without them, the need for shifting angles and distance quickly, in accordance with parrying rather than blocking with the hands, requires a narrower and more upright stance when on guard. In illegal boxing matches without gloves today, you still see many fighters in an upright position, and they usually win more often than those in a more crouched stance. The stance gives you the greatest reach for straight punches and a better platform for leaning away and parrying, but it has its drawbacks, too. It makes the fighter more vulnerable to attacks to the mark, and it makes dodging and ducking more difficult.

In this position, the legs are straighter and the body leans away from the opponent, with the weight on the rear leg. The hands are staggered, with the left leading and the right held across the body. The illustration in *The Art of Boxing* shows a pronounced bend in the wrists, but it is doubtful this was the case in real matches; if we look at other illustrations, the wrists are always held straight to avoid injuries. The front hand is held at shoulder height and the rear hand at the nipple.

In Thomas Fewtrell's work *Boxing Reviewed*, published in 1790, we find yet another form of guard attributed to Thomas Johnson. [1] This is an altogether different guard, more similar to Mendoza's than any other. It is probably a variation of Mendoza's crouch, but with the upper body angled in so it faces more to the front.

19

Thomas Johnson in a guard position, from *Boxing Reviewed, or the Science of Manual Defence*, 1790.

Johnson's stance has the feet almost square, with the legs bent and the upper body bent sharply forward at the waist. Weight is evenly distributed between the feet. The hands are held in front of the face at equal distance from the head. This stance was recommended to pugilists who had great strength in the legs, and it supposedly was rather decent, being equally suited to defense and offense. But Fewtrell points out that few used it in his day.

Edmund Price advocates something in between them all. He stands upright, with a slight bend in the knees, and holds his hands at chest height, leading with the left and guarding with the right. This gives him cover, reach, and mobility. It is also a rather natural stance to be in, which is essential to self-defense, where anything contrived will cause you problems once you get the adrenaline dump in a conflict situation.

Ulf demonstrating Johnson's stance.

Side view.

Price's basic guard position.

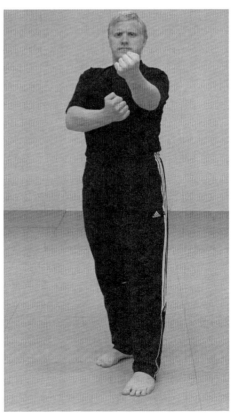

LEFT: Front view.

RIGHT: Side view.

This is a good stance when you fight for real rather than for points or technical knockout, and let us consider why. When you don't wear gloves, it becomes of paramount importance to avoid getting hit. Simply parrying an attack, rather than avoiding it altogether, will let the opponent keep the initiative and attack again. What does this have to do with a narrow stance? A narrower stance enables you to move faster and change the angle of attack easier and more often than you can with a large, deep stance. (The importance of this concept of angling will become apparent as we discuss deflection and counterattacks.) The value of the hand position also becomes apparent: if you do not wear gloves, you can't hide behind them and use them for blocking, period. It is that simple—without gloves, you must use the hands and arms to deflect attacks or avoid them altogether. In modern boxing, on the other hand, it is often the glove itself that is used almost as a shield. It is a radical difference, and it is the reason why the ordinary boxing stance is not that good, in our and the historical masters' opinion, in a self-defense/fighting situation. It is adapted for an athletic contest and not primarily for self-defense, and it should be evaluated for its utility in the ring and nothing else.

Leading with one hand as opposed to holding both at a more or less equal distance from the body is beneficial for many reasons. First, it keeps the opponent at bay somewhat; if he wants to close in, he must negotiate your lead hand or else he will get hit in the face with it. (We will deal later with the fine art of making a true left-hand strike rather than a weak jab, which is good if your aim is to score points in a 12-round match but less so in a real fight that may be over in seconds.) The front hand is also a first line of defense with which to set an incoming attack aside and, through that, open an angle into the opponent.

The rear hand is held close to the body and often at breast height. The arm is relaxed but the fist is tensed, creating a slight tension between the shoulder blades, which is essential for all explosive muscular movement. The arm is pulled back as far as conveniently possible while still providing protection. From that position, it is used to strike or deflect an attack to the head or body.

We now have a guard position that is working. Feet are slightly less than shoulder-width apart, toes toward the opponent, weight of the body more on the toes than the heels, left arm held out, and the right close to the body at chest height. A variation found in the twilight years of the bare-knuckle era had the lead hand out almost straight, with the rear hand cocked for a punch. This is actually a decent stance, with some very interesting points.

A rather special skill that was stressed by the bare-knuckle boxers was that you should be able to lead with either hand. This means you must train to be ambidextrous in your fighting. It can be very effective to confuse the opponent by suddenly switching sides, but in doing so from the variation stance described above, you can also quickly torque your hips and strike with your cocked rear hand to the opponent's now open side. So the guard must be practiced on both sides, as must smoothly changing sides. It gives you the ability to actually step and punch with either foot and hand, which is of great use in a real self-defense situation.

Greek black-figure amphora depicting two boxers. Notice the similarity of the guard position with that advocated by Mendoza; clearly he was not the first to use it. It was probably one of several in use at the time that had been handed down since antiquity.

Significantly, examples of the guard stance can be seen in the ancient world as well. There are some very interesting illustrations of boxers in the exact same type of high stance, with the hands positioned the same way. In Rome, for example, we see the same guard being used by the *caestus* boxers. The usefulness of these guards, therefore, can be said to have been understood early, and they survived probably for the simple reason that they worked.

The orientation of the hands in bare knuckle is interesting since it differs slightly from modern boxing. In bare knuckle, it was considered a good idea to hold one or more hands with the palms facing up rather than toward each other, as is common today. The rear hand was, however, often held in a vertical position, with the palm facing in.

To understand the position of the front hand, we must consider how a punch is deflected. An incoming straight punch is deflected upward by lifting the lead hand. This is also one of the reasons why it is held low; that way, it more easily travels upward in a straight line. If I hold my hands below my face, then I know I will deflect upward whatever comes in above my hands. If I hold my hands in front of my face—and without gloves to duck behind—I will have to choose whether to deflect an incoming blow up or down. In a fight, it is important to minimize the amount of decision making that takes place. Having few choices is a good choice!

How to Hit Properly

It demands great skill and a lot of training to be able to throw a punch, with all your might and weight, at someone's head and have something resembling a fist left afterwards. Conditioning the hands to do this is dealt with in a separate chapter. We begin here with which part of the hand should connect with the opponent's anatomy, and how to do it properly.

The human hand is fragile. Modern-day boxers can pummel away the way they do because their hands are bandaged and they wear solid gloves that fix the hand and wrist into a tight, rigid package. As Jack Dempsey points out in the first two chapters of his book, there has been a watering down of the knowledge of hitting hard in boxing and his aim in the book is to recify this. This does not mean that boxers do not hit hard, because they do. Dempsey meant that when "boxing" in self-defense, you must hit correctly or you will destroy your hand with one punch. You also must have conditioned your hands for gloveless punching. Both these issues must be addressed if the hands are going to be useful in self-defense. There is no point in throwing a punch and not being able to throw another because you struck so poorly that you broke your fingers, knuckles, or wrist. (In fact, if you watch a modern boxing match in slow motion, it becomes very clear that punches often impact randomly on the fist.)

The first skill is clenching the fist properly. To clench the fist, pull the fingers in and close the thumb. Clench

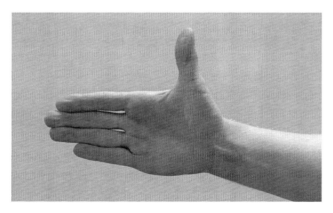

Making a proper fist. From here . . .

. . . curl the fingers.

Clench the fist.

Tuck the thumb.

as tightly as you can without tightening the arm, as doing that will make you slow and clumsy. This means that your fist is closed but not squeezed shut.

When boxers punch, it is often done with the middle of the fist. This works well when wearing gloves, but if you try that without gloves you will break your knuckles. To understand the proper bare-knuckle strike, you must understand the anatomy of the hand.

The striking surface of a clenched hand is shaped like a slope, with the upper knuckles protruding the furthest. The trick is not to strike with the most protruding knuckles. In bare knuckle, you want to strike with the largest and flattest surface in order to spread the force of the impact over a larger area of the fist. That means you want to hit with the three *lowest* knuckles—the pinkie, the ring finger, and the middle finger to be precise—and you aim with the ring finger knuckle.

The hand pulled upward, aligning the bottom knuckles with the arm.

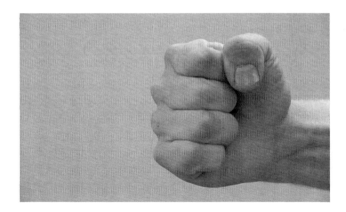

The fist seen from the front inside, twisting the wrist upward in order to extend the lowest three knuckles and giving you a large, flat area with which to impact.

This was common knowledge in earlier days. Jack Dempsey writes about it in *Championship Fighting*, [2] where he also introduces the last important aspect of striking with this part of the hand. In order to hit effectively with the bottom knuckles of a clenched fist, you must pull the hand upward so those knuckles align with the outstretched arm.

The three lowest knuckles impacting on target.

Striking with the bottom knuckles enables the entire arm to absorb the kinetic energy of the strike.

If you look at what happens to the force if we connect with an incorrect fist, we see something very interesting. As you know from basic physics, any force is counteracted by an equal force in the opposite direction. This means that if I hit your face with 20kg of force, then 20kg of force is projected back into my striking fist, which is why people break things in their hand when they strike incorrectly. If you strike with the uppermost part of the fist, the line of force will actually go back and leave your arm before reaching the elbow, leaving you with less mass behind the punch to absorb this force.

By striking with the bottom part of the fist, you get a straight line to the elbow and then to the shoulder. It is simple proof that, based on basic biomechanical principles, the old way of striking is superior. It offers the most solid line to absorb the kinetic energy of the strike, resulting in an unharmed hand. Striking in this manner (and conditioning the hands properly, covered in chapter 5) will allow for strikes to the head without any difficulty at all.

A second type of strike with the hand is found in a book by a proclaimed pupil of both Mendoza and Humphrey. It is done with the palm, and the target is the ribs. Presumably, this strike was done from a close distance. [3] A palm strike can, of course, be aimed at many other targets on the body. (As a side note, this anonymously authored work is interesting because it claims to show boxing as self-defense and not a sport activity.)

Stepping diagram of the angles and distances in the guard position, from R.G Allanson-Winn's book, *Boxing*.

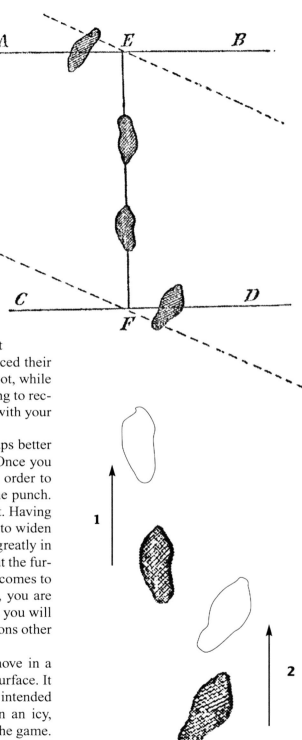

Footwork

Moving in combat is important. The medieval sword master Johannes Liechtenauer said, "That which moves is alive and that which is still is dead."[4] True indeed, and even more so if you have no gloves to cover yourself and no ropes to lean on and the opponent has a friend and both are hell bent on reducing your face to pulp. Under such circumstances, when and soaking up hits to score points is not an option, moving and doing damage to your opponent become of paramount importance.

Considering the rather narrow, high stance that most bare-knuckle boxers seem to recommend, their footwork must have been very quick, with short steps. (A similar high stance can be seen in early photos of karate masters and Chinese martial artists.) With all footwork, the issue of balance is crucial. If we again look at Mendoza and Humphry (page 17), we see they have balanced their bodies differently—Mendoza has the weight on his front foot, while Humphry has his on the rear foot. Both ways have something to recommend them, but it is easier to shift the feet if you stand with your weight on your rear foot.

From a self-defense point of view, however, it is perhaps better to have the weight on the rear leg when in a high stance. Once you step in close to strike, your stance must become wider in order to facilitate the hip torque that is the prime powerhouse of the punch. As you retreat, you must again narrow the stance somewhat. Having your weight on your rear leg not only facilitates the ability to widen and narrow your stance quickly and in balance, but it aids greatly in moving in every direction. We can always move forward, but the further forward you are in your stance, the more difficult it becomes to move in other directions. With the weight on the rear leg, you are more at the point of equilibrium (or slightly behind it), and you will be able to move more quickly and with less effort in directions other than forward.

The following movements cover the basic ways to move in a fight, especially if it takes place on an uneven or slippery surface. It is important to recall that the European martial arts were intended to be used while wearing winter clothes and standing on an icy, badly cobbled street. Simplicity is, therefore, the name of the game. These steps will change a little when they are combined with hand and leg techniques, as they must to accommodate the situation you are facing.

The step.

The Step

This is a simple step forward with the lead foot, and the rear foot follows. To the rear it is reversed: the rear foot moves first and the front foot follows. Neither foot passes the other—the lead foot is maintained moving forward or backward. This step is used to close with the opponent as well as when you want to throw a strong, decisive strike with your lead hand.

This is also the way to sidestep the opponent in order to come in from the side. Your lead foot steps to the side as your body sinks down in the step, and the other foot follows. The attack lands as the foot lands on the ground.

The Pass

The pass is when one of your feet passes the other while moving forward or backward. You use this step when you walk normally, so there is nothing strange about it. Do not strike while passing if you can avoid it, because doing so would result in an unbalanced, slow strike. Rather, the pass is simply a step that takes you to a spot from where you can throw a solid punch.

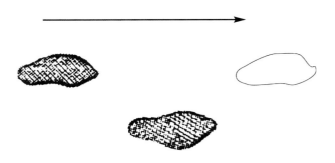

The pass.

Angular Stepping

Done with either leg, angular stepping places you to the outside of the opponent's attack, either forward or backward depending on the situation. Here it is even possible to cross your legs for a brief instant while changing the leading leg.

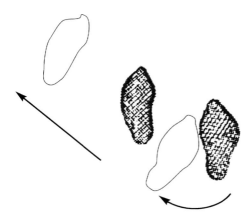

Angular stepping.

27

Flying Out

This concept is found very early in English martial arts literature. It is, for instance, one of the key concepts of George Silver's method of swordsmanship outlined in his writings of the late 16th and early 17th centuries. Flying out is done after you have closed in and made your attack; if you did not take down the opponent, you "fly out" to regroup for the next attack. In boxing, flying out can be taken to mean throwing your body and head backwards. It can be a pass or a shuffle, but do not change the relationship of the feet during the move, i.e., the same foot remains in the lead.

There is no way around this—flying out must be done with agility and speed. This means you need strength, while remaining light on your feet. With training, flying out can be done very explosively and can move your body a significant distance backwards.

TARGET AREAS

Bare-knuckle target areas include most of the body you can conveniently reach. Attacks with the fists connect from the groin up, depending on where you are in the fight. (More on this in chapter 3.) No part of the head or neck is excluded. Attacks with the legs target the opponent's lower legs and up to the groin but never higher. All kicks are done forward, not from the side, and with a straight leg (i.e., no roundhouse kicks). Throws can attack the body, an arm, or the neck, depending on the technique.

The "mark," or solar plexus.

The jaw, struck straight or from below.

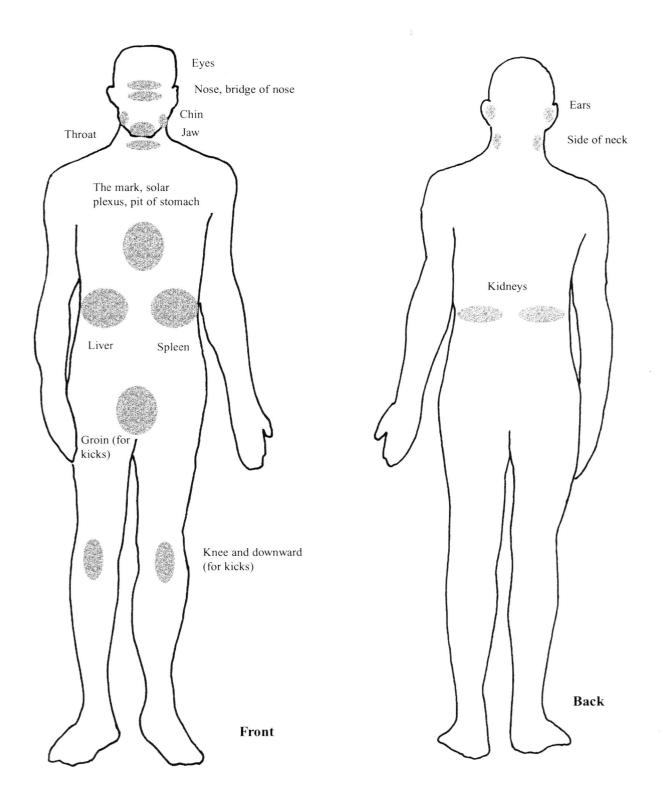

Eyes

Nose, bridge of nose

Chin

Throat   Jaw

The mark, solar
plexus, pit of stomach

Liver   Spleen

Groin (for
kicks)

Knee and downward
(for kicks)

Front

Ears

Side of neck

Kidneys

Back

The chin, struck from the side.

Between the eyes, considered a knockout blow or for cutting the eyebrows.

Lower ribs (floating ribs), struck from the side or front.

Bare-knuckle boxers did not limit their strikes to soft targets, as some people erroneously state today. Favorite targets certainly included soft targets like the pit of the stomach, but they also included the ribs on either side (with the liver shot a favorite), between the eyes, the chin, behind the jaw in front of the ear, the back of the head, the nose, and the mouth. Strikes to the heart were known as well. Striking the bony portion of the head was also an option if that was all that presented itself, but that meant the hands had to be that much more conditioned to withstand the stress.

The kidneys, with the knuckles facing two different ways.

NOTES

1. Fewtrell, *Boxing Reviewed*.
2. Dempsey, *Championship Fighting*.
3. *Boxing Made Easy, or the Complete Manual of Self Defence*, p. 6. (This is likely a reprint of the English work from 1789 printed in London by Kearsley titled, *The Art of Manual Defence, or System of Boxing Perspicuously Explained in a Series of Lessons and Illustrated by Plates*, authored "by a pupil of both Humphreys and Mendoza.")
4. Cod.HS.3227.a. Quote from the so-called Döbringers fechtbuch in translation by David Lindholm, fol.32R (*wer do leit der ist tot / Wer sich ru[e]ret der lebt noch*), http://www.mhfs.se/bibliotek.htm, 26 June 2006.

Chapter

3

BARE-KNUCKLE STRIKES

The strikes that were used in bare-knuckle boxing were basically the same as those seen today in schoolyards across the world. They included a straight strike, round strike, uppercut, and back fist. Some fighters added the low straight kick to the knee and groin, elbow to the head and torso, knee in the groin, and simple hip and neck throws. This is the core arsenal we will cover in this chapter.

The strikes commence from the guard position. This way you avoid cocking the shoulder prior to striking and thus telegraphing intent. The knuckles of your hands should always point toward your opponent—another reason why the guard positions sometimes look a bit differently. Depending on angle and the strike you choose, the path of your strike may change slightly in the heat of the action, but it is important to always try to maintain proper form.

In all strikes, it is very important to strike through and thus true. You do not want to hit *on* something; rather, you want to strike *through* it. In other words, to deliver a hard punch, you must drive through the target when your hand makes contact. The simplest way to accomplish this is to actually aim your hand beyond where you intend to hit.

The next step is withdrawing the hand, and that must be very quick, but many people mistake the two steps and blend them into one. You must not pull your hand back from the target as soon as you connect. The result is a weak punch that is jerked back before it has delivered its damage. You need time on target to be able to punch through it and ultimately deliver a hard strike.

THE STRAIGHT STRIKE

This was considered the most effective of the possible strikes, at least from the basic guard position. It has much to recommend it—your fist travels in a straight line, and by doing so you can defend part of the opening that the strike creates by extending and lifting the arm. Another nice thing about the straight punch is that you can either lean in to the technique for more of a thrust with the fist, or you can punch while keeping the body back. (Basically it is the same movement, but with different application of the body. The latter is closer to the modern jab, while the former will knock someone out cold if it lands solidly.) The straight punch can be delivered from the side or head on, depending on the situation. All this, along with the capacity for maintaining good balance and focus, is why the bare-knuckle masters considered the straight punch was superior to other types of strikes with the hands.

When throwing a straight strike, it was recommended that you do so with the hand positioned vertical rather then horizontal. This has to do with the power line discussed in the previous chapter, which is easier to maintain if the hand is vertical. Not that a horizontal fist will not work, but as Dempsey says, and as is illustrated in peri-

Straight strike on the same side as the leading foot. The body moves slightly forward on both feet; shoulder is high.

Straight strike, same leg and hand, stepping in as you strike to get the whole body behind it.

Straight strike on the opposite leg side. This has shorter reach and is best done after closing in.

Straight strike on the opposite leg, this time holding the body back.

Same strike, but this time leaning into it.

A straight strike to the mark, opposite hand and foot, without leaning into the strike too much for fast withdrawal.

od manuals of the day, a vertical fist allows for a completely straight line from the knuckles through the wrist, elbow, and shoulder without any bends or kinks in it. If you do not have wraps or gloves, this becomes of paramount importance.

THE ROUND STRIKE

Round strikes were well known and understood, but they were considered by bare knucklers to have limited use in a real fight. This attitude was mainly based on fencing theory relating to the small sword, and to the rapier before that. It stated that any cut (which in this case would have been synonymous with a round strike) will arrive later than a straight thrust. This theory could be verified through geometry, but the real reason round strikes were not favored by bare knucklers may have been because they left you vulnerable. A round strike's swinging motion requires you to commit the body for the strike to have any power. This will put you in motion in such a way that you will not be able to react to any opposing movement or attack until your technique is complete, leaving you open to all sorts of counters.

Because they increase your risk of getting hit, round strikes are not used as a closing attack in bare knuckle. They are used, however, as a counterattack to an opponent's closing attack. The counter is usually done to the outside of the opponent's arms.

The Hook

There is scarce material on the proper way to throw a hook; most old bare-knuckle manuals focus exclusively on straight strikes and back fists. Typical, sloppy hooks consisting of flailing arms do little to increase damage; a proper hook has your body weight behind it. Throwing a solid hook is a matter of locking the elbow at an angle and violent twisting the body at the waist. The arm remains more or less stationary as it hooks toward the target. The smaller the angle in the elbow, the more the strike becomes a round strike. An acute angle enables you to hook very hard indeed.

In throwing a hook, it is important that you do not strike with the arm only but with the body behind it. Try to deliver the hook either in a slightly rising or falling motion, i.e., start from below and drive your body weight up with it, or from above so you in a sense sit down a little as you strike, putting your weight into the technique. It is certainly possible to throw knockout punches this way.

A hook can be delivered low to the sides of the body and high at the head and face. After blocking a strike at your ribs, for instance, your arm is perfectly placed for a hook to the opponent's body. Hooks can also be done to great effect when the opponent throws a straight punch and misses—say if you sidestep his strike and then hook to the kidneys or floating ribs or over his arm at his head and face.

This is the kind of swing that the masters warn against. It takes time and leaves you open.

This is a more proper form of hook, with the arm held close to the body and delivered from very short range. Observe that the elbow on the striking arm should be a bit lower.

A hook delivered more from below rather than the side.

THE UPPERCUT

The uppercut is another close-in attack that does not lend itself well as an opening move. The body rises into the strike by driving up with the legs. The fist is held at roughly 45 degrees, giving you the ability to aim with the lower knuckles and strike with the correct power line.

As far as I know, there is not a single mention of the uppercut in a bare-knuckle text prior to the late 19th or early 20th century, when stances and guards changed to accommodate gloves and rules. The fact is that if you rely on the recommended guard positions and bare-knuckle strikes, and if you include such moves as throws and head butts in your arsenal, the uppercut becomes of limited use. I am convinced that it was used in bare knuckle, but it would have been of limited importance due to these factors. Mendoza does mention a form of uppercut (or it can be understood as such) after blocking a blow to the mark, as do other writers, but it is not categorized as a strike on its own.

THE BACK FIST

The back fist, or chopper, is used to attack an opponent after you have parried one of his attacks. It is a counter or a continuation of an attack already under way; it is not an opening

A standard form of uppercut delivered at close range.

LEFT: A simple downward back fist aimed at the bridge of the opponent's nose.

RIGHT: This is similar to what today usually goes under the name of hammerfist. A chopper easily turns into this kind of strike from certain angles, but as far as I know it was not recognized as a separate strike. It is, however, rather useful in the arsenal.

move. Very difficult to defend against if done well, it was a favorite attack of Daniel Mendoza, but others were not so enthusiastic about its efficiency. It is perhaps safest to say that it offers a quick, relatively safe return strike after performing a successful parry, and this makes it an important part of your arsenal. It can be done from any high parry; low parries provide better avenues of countering. In striking a back fist, you flick the knuckles downward in a dragging motion that goes across the opponent's face from above to below. It is not a downward diagonal strike to his face; there is a big difference.

The back fist can, of course, be thrown at other times as well, but that is more often turned into our next technique.

THE BACKSWING

This is something you could do if you happen to miss with a proper hook or a wild, poorly done swing. (Never swing at all if you can avoid it—it was seen as the mark of an amateur.) Directly from the position you end up in after a missed hook, swing your arm backwards, aiming it high toward the opponent's head. Impact can be made with any part of the arm, but if you consider the line of power, you will realize that hitting with the knuckles will probably hurt you more than him. A better option is to hit with the bony underside of the arm just below the elbow. Avoid hitting with the elbow proper, as this will give you a restricted swing and less power. The trick to making the backswing powerful is to relax as much as possible and twist the hips strongly as you swing; do not swing with the arm alone.

THE HEAD BUTT

A classic, but often performed in the wrong way. It is not the same as hitting a football with your head. (That's a soccer ball for you American readers.) To do a good head butt, you must be close to the opponent. Keep your head *still* and step into him by falling forward with your body. That way the impact will carry the entire body weight and not just what you get from nodding your head a bit. You should connect with the uppermost part of the forehead. A head butt can also be done to the side, of course, or backwards as illustrated in medieval German texts. In those cases, you again want to make impact with the hardest, bony portion of the skull.

Standard head butt delivered by using the body and not swinging the head back and forth.

THE TRIP

This technique is done by stepping in on the opponent's outside, preferably of his lead foot, and locking your own foot behind his. With your arms and body working in unison, push him over your leg, preferably using both hands, and twist his body toward his outside as you throw him in order to take away his balance. This works very well in a clinch or wrestling situation.

To counter a trip if someone does it to you, step back with your rear leg and sink down to widen your base. This solidifies your stance and gives you time to counter his attack. [1]

As David on the left steps in to strike, Ulf sets up and behind his heel to trip him.

Ulf trips David by locking his foot behind the heel and driving him backward.

THE CROSS BUTTOCK OR OVER-THE-HIP THROW

An old-school throw. The fighter on the right steps in behind the opponent's lead leg (this is essential) and pushes his opposite shoulder, forcing him back and over. The elbow to the face may be the entry technique that enabled him to move in, or it may be an aid to move the opponent backwards.

This throw was taught as part of the old style of bare knuckle. It is a simple throw over your hip, with your arm gripping the opponent around either the waist or neck. The good thing about this technique is that it is very easy to do once you get in to close fighting distance. If you secure a hold around the opponent's neck, you can finish him by suddenly and violently throwing him by the neck alone. No matter how you do it, the aim is to drop him on his head or neck and *not* on his back.

A more serious variation is to throw him by the neck and maintain your hold. This will damage or snap his neck if you pull forcefully up and back as he flies over and down. Obviously, such a move is only for situations when your life is in danger.

It is important to understand that you must step in aggressively to accomplish the cross buttock; do not wait for him to come to you. The step in needs to be done behind his lead rather than rear leg. This is the only way to quickly gain both a solid hold and an opening for destroying his balance. As you step in, use your shoulder on the side of the catching arm to

A hip throw done from the outside.

A hip throw from the side. Push him forward and take his balance prior to throwing him. When applying this hold, start with a swinging hook that circles the opponent's neck or side.

THE CHANCERY

This is a nice technique that simply entails capturing the opponent's head underneath one of your arms and pummeling him with your other fist. What is less known about the chancery is that it is relatively easy to apply after you parry a strike due to the positioning of your and the opponent's arms. If, for instance, the opponent steps in with a straight punch at your face and you defend by parrying it upward, simply take a small step forward and extend your arm until it lands on the opponent's shoulder. If you hook the arm in the same motion, you will catch his head in the chancery. If you think of how often boxers go into clinch, then you can understand how easy it is to catch the opponent's head. Just remember that catching his head is an aggressive forward move and does not entail simply taking hold of him limply. Once you have him locked up, pull his head close and twist your body away from his body. This will torque his body and neck and make it much more difficult for him to escape.

Getting Out of the Chancery

The basic idea for escaping a chancery holds true for any type of hold around the neck or head. The first issue is to avoid getting hit in the face or choked out. In order to do that, one hand must be set aside to counter the attack. If your opponent has your head or upper body in a hold using both his hands, do not waste time trying to unlock his arms or hands. Either punch as hard as you can at his liver several times, or strike his chin as hard as you can from below with the palm of your hand. If you can reach, push your thumb into one of his eyes as hard and fast as you can. If you do it slowly, he can actually squeeze his eye shut enough to prevent you from hurting him badly. You can also dig the knuckles in and gouge his eyes, an old favorite of the bare-knuckle era.

If you are in a true chancery, place the hand on your opponent's far side in front of your face to guard it. Dig your chin into his waist to guard your face even more and prevent him from choking you. The other hand goes up the opponent's back and in front of his face. Then push his head sideways and back to throw him over your leg.

Ulf has locked David's head in the chancery and pulls him close to be able to control and strike him.

David escapes the chancery by reaching up and over Ulf's shoulder with the arm closest to Ulf and pulls/presses his head and face rearward. As David raises himself up to standing, he uses the power of the legs to push Ulf backwards and down.

THE PARRIES

The ways to deflect attacks seem to have remained rather consistent throughout the history of pugilism. On Greek vases we see the same defenses against strikes as were recommended in later bare-knuckle instructions. This is perhaps not so strange after all, since human anatomy hadn't changed, there are few basic movements that really work, and intelligent people figured them out at an early date. In the old bare-knuckle texts, the parries were coupled with the specific attack they were intended to counter; therefore, here we give the parry and the attack as one unit.

Blocking a straight strike. The left figure blocks the strike by lifting his arm.

Blocking a strike with the opposite hand.

Blocking a strike with the opposite hand, apparently by pushing it to the outside. He might be lifting it up, but the image is distorted due to problems with depicting foreshortened parts of the body correctly.

43

Parrying the Straight Punch

The straight punch is aimed at the face. It does not matter if the impact point is the nose, mouth, chin, or eyebrow—the parry works regardless of target. The basic idea—as described in, for instance, *Boxing Made Easy*—is that you lift your arm up and a bit out to deflect the incoming strike with your forearm. [2] This is an easy defense that works surprisingly well.

Both Mendoza and the author of *Boxing Made Easy* recommend that you parry with the arm on the same side of the attack. That is, if the opponent strikes at your face with his left hand, you parry with your right. We have tried to parry everything with the lead hand regardless of which side the attacks are aimed, and it works. There are, however, differences in the possible follow-ups that can be done.

When parrying, it is recommended that you lift your elbow as high as the rest of your arm so you have a horizontal bar just above your head.

We start in a guard position. Here we use a more upright guard than, for instance, Mendoza seems to have done.

Ulf steps and punches at David's face, who parries with the same hand as the strike, which is the left. This opens up the opponent's outside for a counter.

Here David parries with the same side as the strike but not the same hand—that is, Ulf strikes with the left and David defends with the right. This opens up the centerline for a counter.

44

Parrying the Round Strike

The round strike in any form did not have a good reputation in the bare-knuckle era. The reason was said to be that a round strike took longer to reach its target, and it was that much more difficult to perform with power. It opened you up while providing a small return on your investment, so to speak. That said, it was used in bouts, and we surmise that the original discontent with this technique stemmed from the fact that a bad swing is too easily countered (a good hook, however, is another matter). In all likelihood, this view indicates that infighting at close distance was not that popular with bare-knuckle fighters. One reason might be that they were wary of throws and locks, which were allowed during bouts. Such techniques end fights soon, as we know from watching K-1 and similar events today.

Parrying a round strike is simple. It is done by either raising the elbow forward and up, catching the strike on the outside of the arm, or by lifting the elbow sideways, catching the strike on the side or underside of the arm. Essentially, it is more of a stop than the front-strike parry, which is more of an upward redirection of the attack.

Ulf strikes round at David, who parries by lifting the elbow and catching the strike. The parry can either stop the strike or lift it over to the opposite side.

The fighter on the right throws a round strike at the face, which his opponent blocks by raising the elbow. The attacker follows with a blow to the mark, which is defended by barring it.

A variation on the parry against a round strike, where the elbow is lifted, catching the strike on the arm. Seen in Sullivan's text from 1893 and still in use in modern boxing, this version also works well.

The fighter on the right stops the blow by catching it on his bent right arm.

DEFENDING THE MARK AND THE SIDES

Hitting the mark—the solar plexus, described as the "pit of the stomach" to indicate the depression between the ribcage—was considered to be of primary importance. The reason was simply that most people can't take a hit with a bare fist there without going down.

Defending the mark could be done in two ways. The first was by barring, which meant simply placing your rearmost arm across the mark and letting the opponent hit it. The second possibility was to strike the opponent's attacking arm with your own. This has the added benefit of hurting the opponent as well, possibly disabling him for a few seconds if you do it well, and opening him for a strike from below.

Ulf strikes at David's stomach, who bars with his right arm (it hurts, let me tell you).

Ulf strikes with his other hand and David strikes his hand down using the bony part of his own wrist. This hurts Ulf quite a bit and pulls him slightly forward, opening him for David's counter.

The fighter on the right strikes first high at the face and then low at the mark. The first strike is blocked by lifting it up and the second by barring the mark. Notice how close to each other they stand.

Ulf strikes at David's sides, who defends by pulling down the elbow.

In order to defend the sides of the body (i.e., kidneys and sides of the ribcage), you simply pull down the elbow sharply, keeping it in contact with your body to act as a shield.

KICKING

Kicking is not an expressed part of the bare-knuckle manuals, but it can be inferred that it was done since it was eventually prohibited, as was using the knees (among other things). Therefore, we would like to present a few simple kicks that can be found in earlier European material dating from the Middle Ages and Renaissance.

Kicks are aimed low (i.e., below the groin) simply because it is difficult to kick higher with efficiency in a real-life situation and when wearing normal clothing. Deliver them a bit like savate kicks, with a rather straight leg driven forward and without leaning over with the body. Kick using the bottom or tip of the foot, but remember that shoes do help!

Ulf kicks David with the bottom of the foot.

Ulf kicks with the bottom of the foot at David's shin—a useful technique when the opponent closes in.

Ulf kicks David above the knee with the tip of the foot.

GIVING THE RETURN

Although the author of *Boxing Made Easy* claims "giving the return" to be an invention of Mendoza, we know this is not the case because the concept was shown in sword texts from the Middle Ages. Mendoza does, however, describe this tactic in his book. Basically, the idea is that as you parry, you must simultaneously launch a counterattack. If you do not do this, your opponent will control the development of combat and you will most likely lose. To give the return also means that you should not do your movements in a predictable, 1-2 pattern or rhythm, which will give the opponent time to rearrange his defenses after his attack or attacks. Instead, you must counter immediately, in the quickest way possible, and with conviction and force. The return may also come in the form of chopper attack that is not that forceful but perhaps is quick. In any case, it is of paramount importance that you always counter when attacked and not just sit there and take it. The medieval master Johannes Liechtenauer said that it was essential to strive for the first strike (*Vorschlag*), but if that failed then the "after strike" (*Nachschlag*) absolutely had to be gained. Initiative must be retaken, and this is nothing else then the "return" of the bare-knuckle boxers. Same concept, different terminology.

ADDITIONAL TECHNIQUES FROM SULLIVAN

James Sullivan's book from 1893 on boxing as self-defense contains much interesting material. The following is a selection of his techniques to complement the previous material. Sullivan is relevant for the same reason as Price: he stands at the crossroads of the bare-knuckle martial art and the modern sport of boxing, and as such his recommendations are more likely to reflect the earlier, tested techniques and ideas that had not yet been adapted to the ring.

Sullivan starts with some general, sound advice. First, he says, always strike using the body rather than with the strength of the arms alone. Always make sure your strikes connect, even if it risks a counter, with the motivation that it will teach you to hit faster and guard better next time.

Sullivan considered footwork important. The weight should be evenly placed, the front foot pointed at the opponent, the rear foot cocked out at 45 degrees or so, and the distance between the front heel and rear toes about 12–15 inches. The rear heel should be raised a little, the knees slightly bent. As you work on your opponent, strive toward your right side since you then move away of his right hand.

The body should be turned a quarter away from the opponent, with the rear shoulder lower than the front, giving you an inclining posture. Keep the eyes focused on the opponent's eyes, and be sure your tongue is not lodged between the lips or teeth so you don't bite it during the action. Keep moving the head, and feel the body as being light and mobile. Counter to either side, and do so with the hand on the same side as the incoming strike so your counter comes in from his outside. Never duck without hitting back.

Sullivan has interesting suggestions on timing. When the opponent advances, extend the left hand halfway and withdraw the right. It should be done easy and slight. This allows you to keep the time of the opponent, positioning yourself so you can anticipate his advance and prepare a timely counterstrike. When the opponent steps in to attack, he must move in to cover the distance, and that's when you use timing to your advantage. In retreating, you lure or pull the opponent further into his attack until he has gone too far and overextended himself. This is when you counter with ease. (In tai chi, there is a saying that when the opponent advances the distance is surprisingly long, yet when I advance, the distance is surprisingly short.)

Guard Position

Stand with your feet some 15 inches apart and with the heels in line. The right hand arm should be held across the ribs, with the finger knuckles in front of or touching the left breast. The left should be extended in line with your elbow and your opponent's face.

Both fighters in the guard position.

Right Hand Guard for the Body

To guard against a strike to the body, whip your arm down and out to sweep the blow aside. When the opponent tries to strike at your body, he will be forced to bend forward and down to some extent, so it is also possible to stop him by delivering a straight punch to the face as he comes forward.

The guard with the right hand, seen from both sides. David's left hand is being extended in preparation for an uppercut.

Countering with the left hand.

Left Hand Counter

Here, David deflects a left strike to the face and counters at once with a left to Ulf's face. It is essential to move both arms simultaneously. Lean forward slightly to the side you are countering on to put weight behind the counter. This works well on either side.

Duck/Step with a Left Hand Counter to the Face

When the opponent strikes at you with a straight punch, move your head and upper body forward to your right so his strike passes over your left shoulder; then, step in with either the rear or front foot (maintaining the same footing), and counter to his face. You are also in a perfect position to strike his ribs.

If you want to guard yourself from this counter, duck outside to your right at the same time as your opponent and/or push the counterpunch sideways with your right hand.

Left Hand Guard and Right Hand Counter

This is a useful technique against an opponent who tends to swing slightly toward the opposite side when throwing a straight. You deflect his strike with the same hand (e.g., left versus left), which will turn him further and expose his side and ribs. Counter with a strike to the ribs, leaning in with the body as you strike. Raise your guarding arm slightly higher than usual.

David has stepped forward with the rear foot in the counter. (In the original illustration it is a shuffle step, leading with the same foot.) To put weight behind the counter, allow the body to come in behind the strike.

David deflects with his left and counters to the face with his right.

Left Hand Guard and Right Hand Counter

Ulf strikes at David with a right and David guards with the left. As he does so, David strikes at Ulf's face, throwing his shoulder forward in order to engage the body and avoid a limp arm strike. As usual, this can be done on either side.

Ulf deflects with his left and counters to the ribs with his right.

Right Hand Cross Counter

When the opponent strikes at you with a left, bend slightly forward at the waist and duck a bit out to the left side. Strike over the opponent's arm with your right, hitting him in the face. This strike often becomes more of a swing since you must cross over the opponent's lead arm. Don't be too quick here—it is almost as if you are allowing him to hit you. If you are too quick, your intentions will be easy to read and counter. As you connect, turn your feet slightly toward the side that the strike is traveling in order to get the body really into it. Follow up with a left to the face or body as you see an opening. This works against a right as well, but you should lead with the other hand or switch stance.

If you see a cross counter coming, move your head forward and touch the inside of your arm to your ear. That way the strike will pass over your head. It also gives you a solid opening for a counter. You can also guard in the old style by withdrawing the left arm a bit and raising the elbow, which also offers the opportunity for a good counter. Finally, if you anticipate this move, you can preempt it by hitting him in the chest or near the attacking shoulder.

Right hand cross counter, seen from both sides.

This shows stopping a cross counter by halting the opponent's body with a solid straight to the chest. This counter is useful as a general way of impeding the opponent's advance. You can employ it with several forms of stepping and ducking.

Left Hand Uppercut

The uppercut lends itself well against, for instance, a straight strike from the left. As the opponent strikes, you counter with your left from below. It doesn't matter which strike the opponent uses, but the uppercut should come in across the body and move upward. In essence, it is more of a counter rather than an attack since it has less reach and depends on the opponent first coming to you. Uppercuts as strikes are always done from a close range.

Right Hand Uppercut to the Outside

This strike is executed as a counter when the opponent uppercuts. Lean the body slightly to the outside as you strike. Do not turn it into a horizontal swing by launching it from too far out to the side.

Ulf counters with an uppercut to David's chin.

David counters Ulf's uppercut by coming in from the outside.

Duck and Counter for an Uppercut

When the opponent strikes at you with an uppercut, duck toward the outside and strike at once. Here, David has simultaneously taken a step forward as he counters to the body. If you remain stationary with the feet, simply lean toward the side opposite of his strike since that will be both open and safe. A counter to the body will be most natural, even though a counter to the head also works well.

David ducks and counters Ulf's uppercut from the outside.

54

Chancery

If your hand passes over your opponent's as you strike, wrap your hand around his neck and pull forward to execute a chancery. Cock your free hand while holding him tight; then pull his head toward you as you drive a punch into his face.

When using the chancery, try to avoid clinging to the opponent too long. You really only want one or, at best, two solid punches to the face; then be prepared to let him go. If you cling to him, it can be used against you since this grip can easily be turned into a trip or fall.

Ulf locks David in a chancery and prepares to punch.

Getting Out of the Chancery

When the opponent has you around the neck, you need to get away quickly. The fastest way is to push him away while simultaneously creating a barrier for a counterstrike. Lift your free arm up and strike/push the opponent's head away.

David's left arm creates a guard against a counterstrike as he forcefully pushes Ulf away to escape the chancery.

The other chancery, seen from both sides.

Another Form of Chancery

This is another version of the chancery, executed when the opponent steps in with a lead and then ducks left as you counter. Lock your arm around his neck and draw his head down and to the right, opening him up for an attack to his ribs. This is a more solid grip then the previous chancery; remember, however, that just as you can strike at his exposed ribs to great effect, so can he do some serious damage to you from this position, especially in a self-defense situation were there are no rules.

Getting Out of the Chancery

Since this hold is inverted, it is much more difficult to extract yourself, especially since the opponent is striking at your ribs. To get out, forcefully shove his head with your right hand and his body with your left. The right pushes back and up on the jaw; the left pushes at the hip, since that joint is hard to keep rigid when attacked. Push the hip back and away and the body will follow.

David escapes the inverted chancery with an explosive shove to Ulf's head and body.

Ulf executes a back fall against David.

Back Fall

A marked difference between the older forms of bare knuckle and the modern sport was that throws and tripping were allowed in the former. This is, of course, especially interesting from a self-defense perspective, where a rudimentary grasp of throwing techniques is a must.

To execute this back fall, rush in close to the opponent and throw your left arm around his waist and right arm under his chin. As you step in, try to place your left leg behind his right. The throw is done by pushing him back under the chin while maintaining your hold around his waist. It might seem odd, but the arm around the waist prevents him from moving backward to regain balance. Once his balance is gone, simply continue to push, but release the waist and down he goes.

Countering a Back Fall

To counter a back fall, you must first immobilize the arm around your waist by locking it to your body with the arm on the same side. This will put pressure on the opponent's arm and elbow joint. With your other hand, push the arm under the chin up and a bit sideways, preferably by applying pressure at the elbow joint. Proceeding from this point is more difficult, since both your hands are engaged. Striking is not a top priority, but executing your own back fall might work, or simply disengage and deliver a straight strike to his face.

Ulf attempts a back fall against David.

David locks Ulf's left arm to his body and shoves his right at the elbow.

By maintaining pressure on the elbow and pushing forward, David executes his own back fall against Ulf.

The back hip fall, seen from both sides.

Back Hip Fall

This is a very good throw that allows for a quick end to a fight. The opponent leads with a left, and you step out and duck to your right. As you rush in, throw your left arm around his waist and step in with your left leg well behind him. Place the right hand under his chin, raise him on your hip, and throw him over with force, using both hands for leverage.

NOTES

1. Allanson-Winn, *Boxing*, pp. 50–51.
2. *Boxing Made Easy, or the Complete Manual of Self Defence*, p. 7.

Chapter
4

BARE-KNUCKLE PRACTICE PATTERNS

It seems that much bare-knuckle training that was not done in the form of sparring consisted of set patterns, a mode of working with combative arts well documented both in Europe and Asia. It is a simple, safe, and extremely effective way of internalizing movements, responses, and attitudes. Patterns have the added benefit of taking the practitioner to a decent level of proficiency much quicker than other forms of training. Yet another benefit is that you can easily do patterns alone if necessary simply by shadow boxing.

We have decided to include a number of practice patterns from the most accessible master text, that of Daniel Mendoza. This is not a complete list of Mendoza's patterns; rather, our intention is to show you the ones that contain the most basic material covered in his book so you can clearly see how to train in bare knuckle. We have, however, included all unillustrated patterns as text so you can work them out on your own if you wish.

You can also find great patterns and exercises in the works of Sullivan and Price. The value of the patterns of Mendoza and his pupils lies less in the excellence of the patterns as in the fact that they provide historical, easy-to-follow sets of movements on which you can easily base and construct your own.

The terms "Master" and "Scholar" are an old way of designating the two parties in any practice sequence. The master takes the role of the knowledgeable teacher, while the scholar is the young man learning the art. You can think of it as the *uke* and *tori* in Japanese arts.

Do not try to copy Mendoza's way of doing these patterns exactly. Rather, use his methods as a starting point and find what suits your training needs. Virtually the same patterns are found in the works of other authors who advocated different styles and guards. In that sense, these patterns seem to have been used as a general training regimen rather than as a unique Mendoza system. Then again, his text appears to be the first to contain them, so perhaps he created the patterns later used by others. In any case, they a good foundation for training in bare knuckle, so they work well for our purposes.

When practicing the patterns, execute them carefully. Do not do them quickly and become sloppy. Practice slow and learn fast.

In all these patterns, you can use many different forms of footwork. We have opted to not try to show overly active footwork since it takes away from the clarity of the strikes and blocks.

Note that when lifting the opponent's arm—especially when you perform the forearm parry—you will lift him up and in essence unbalance him as he extends. Also notice how both Ulf and David aim the arm not in use directly at the opponent, ready for an immediate counter strike. This is most clearly visible in Ulf's postures.

61

LESSON 1

Master strikes with his left arm at your face.

Parry with your right forearm, at the same time barring your stomach with your left forearm while throwing your head and body back.

From the guard position . . .

. . . David steps in and strikes at Ulf's face with the left, who parries by lifting his elbow while barring the mark with his other arm.

Master strikes with his right at your face.

Parry with your left forearm, at the same time barring your stomach with your right forearm and throwing your head and body back.

On guard. (The remaining photo sequences will presume to begin from this guard position.)

David steps in and strikes at Ulf with his right. Ulf parries by lifting his elbow while barring the mark with his other arm.

Master strikes round at your right ear with his left.

Parry with your right arm, turning the elbow up to cover the side of the head, barring the stomach with the left forearm, and throwing the head and body back.

David steps in and strikes at Ulf with his left. Ulf lifts the elbow and blocks.

Master strikes round at your left ear with his right.

Parry with your left arm, turning the elbow up to cover the side of the head, barring the stomach with the right forearm, and throwing the head and body back.

David strikes at Ulf from his right. Ulf lifts the elbow to deflect it . . .

. . . and lifts the attacking arm over, as shown here, or stops it, as is most suitable to the situation.

Master strikes at your stomach with his left.

Bar your stomach with your right forearm, keeping your left opposite his nose and throwing your head and body back.

Ulf bars David's strike to the stomach.

He strikes at your stomach with his right.

Bar your stomach with your left forearm, keeping the right opposite his nose and throwing head and body back.

His right strikes at your left side.

Stop the strike with your left elbow, keeping your right fist opposite his nose and throwing head and body back.

Ulf bars David's strike to the stomach.

David steps in and strikes at Ulf's side. He blocks it by pulling down the elbow.

LESSON 2

1, 2

Master feints 1, 2 at your face, first with his left in order to hit you in the face with his right.

Parry first with your right forearm and then with your left forearm, covering the stomach with the right forearm and throwing your head and body back.

David strikes at Ulf's face with his left; he blocks it with the forearm.

David then strikes with the right, which Ulf blocks in the same way.

It is also possible to block diagonally, which places you outside the opponent's main line.

Master feints in the same manner, beginning with his right.

Parry first with your left arm and then with your right forearm, covering the stomach with the left forearm and throwing head and body back.

David strikes at Ulf with his right, who parries it.

David then strikes with the left, which Ulf parries.

He feints left at your stomach, to hit your face with his right.

Bar your stomach with your right forearm and parry the blow to your face with your left forearm, throwing head and body back.

David feints at Ulf's stomach, which Ulf bars.

David then throws the real strike at Ulf's face, which Ulf parries.

He does the same with his right.

Bar your stomach with your left forearm and parry the blow to your face with your right forearm, throwing head and body back.

David strikes at Ulf's stomach, who bars it.

David then strikes at Ulf's face with his left. Ulf parries by lifting it upward.

He feints left at your right side, to hit your face with his right.

Stop the feint with your right elbow and parry his blow to your face with the left forearm, throwing head and body back.

David feints a strike at Ulf's side. He parries by dropping his elbow.

David then strikes at Ulf's face, which Ulf parries.

He does the same with his right.

Stop with your left elbow and parry his blow to your face with the right forearm, throwing head and body back.

David's right strikes at Ulf's side. He parries by dropping the elbow.

David then strikes at Ulf's face with his left, who parries it with his right forearm.

Master strikes 1 at the face, 2 at the stomach, with alternate arms.

Parry the first with the proper forearm and the second with the proper bar; that is, if he strikes with his left at your face and the right at your stomach, parry his left with your right forearm and his right with your left across your stomach. If he strikes first with his right at your face and his left at your stomach, parry his right with your left forearm and his left with your right across your stomach.

David strikes with his left at Ulf's face, who deflects it with the proper parry.

David strikes with the right at Ulf's stomach, and he bars it.

Master strikes 1 at the side and 2 at the stomach.

Parry with the proper arms, first by catching the blow on the proper elbow and then by parrying the blow at the stomach with the proper forearm; that is, if he strikes with his left first, catch it with your right elbow and bar his right with your left across your stomach, and vice versa if he strikes with his right.

David strikes at Ulf's right side. Ulf tucks his right elbow to block it.

David strikes at Ulf's stomach, which Ulf bars.

He strikes at the face 1 and 2 at the side.
Parry each with the proper forearm and elbow.

David strikes at Ulf's face. Ulf parries.

David strikes at Ulf side. Ulf bars.

He strikes at the stomach 1 and 2 at the side.
Bar the first with the proper forearm and catch the other with the proper elbow.

David strikes at Ulf's stomach. Ulf bars the strike.

David strikes at Ulf's side. Ulf catches it on his elbow.

LESSON 3

1, 2, 3

Master strikes with his left at your face 1; with his right at your face 2; and with his left at your stomach 3, the intended blow.

Parry the first with your right forearm, the second with your left forearm, and the third with the right forearm barring your stomach, throwing head and body back.

David strikes at Ulf with a straight left. Ulf parries.

David throws a straight right. Ulf parries.

David strikes at Ulf's stomach. Ulf bars.

Master strikes with his right at your face 1; with his left, 2; and with his right at your stomach 3.
Parry the first with your left forearm, the second with your right forearm, and the third with your left arm, barring your stomach and throwing head and body back.

David throws a straight right at Ulf's face. Ulf parries.

Then a straight left, which Ulf parries.

Then the intended blow at the stomach. Ulf bars.

1, 2, 3 at the Face
Master strikes at your head first with his left; second with his right at your face; and third with his left, the intended blow.

Parry the first with your right, the second with your left, the third with your right, your forearm ultimately covering your stomach while throwing head and body back.

David strikes a left at Ulf's face. Ulf parries.

David strikes with the right. Ulf parries.

With the left again. Ulf parries.

Master strikes with his right at your head 1; with his left at your face 2; and with his right 3, the intended blow.
Parry the first strike with your left; the second with your right; the third with your left, your forearm ultimately covering your stomach while throwing head and body back.

David strikes a straight right at Ulf's face. Ulf parries.

Then with the left. Ulf parries.

And again with the right. Ulf parries.

1, 2, 3 at the Side

Master strikes with his left hand at your head first; with his right second; and his left at your side third, the intended blow.

Parry the first with your right forearm; the second with your left forearm; the third with the right elbow.

David strikes a left. Ulf parries.

Then he strikes with the right. Ulf parries.

A variation. After the third parry, Ulf closes in to execute a cross buttocks throw.

Master strikes with his right at your head first; with his left at your head second; then with his right at your side, the intended blow.

Parry the first with your left forearm; the second with your right forearm; and the third with your left elbow.

First a straight right, which Ulf parries.

David throws a straight left. Ulf parries.

David strikes at Ulf's right side. Ulf parries.

In this variation, Ulf counters by catching David's heel and locking it while pushing him backward with the right arm (which starts as a strike).

LESSON 4
Ripostes

Master's left strikes at your face.

Parry with your right forearm and return at his face with your left, which he catches in his open hand.

David throws a straight left at Ulf's face. Ulf parries.

Ulf throws a straight left in return, which David catches in his hand from the front (variations will come later).

His right strikes at your face.

Parry with your left forearm and return at his face with your right.

David strikes a straight left at Ulf, who parries it.

Ulf returns a straight right. David catches it on the side and moves it sideways. This is a more plausible maneuver than actually catching it from the front. Ulf is open to several counters here.

Master's left strikes at your stomach.

Stop by barring with your right forearm and return at his face with your left, which he catches.

David strikes at Ulf stomach. Ulf bars the strike.

David catches Ulf's counter.

His right strikes at your stomach.

Stop by barring with your left forearm and return at his face with your right.

Master's left strikes at your right side.

Stop by catching the blow on your right elbow, and return at his face with your left.

His right strikes at your left side.

Stop by catching the blow on your left elbow, and return at his face with your right.

Master's left chops at your face.

Parry with your right forearm, and return at his face with your left.

His right does the same.

Parry with your right forearm, and return at his face with your left.

Master's left strikes at your stomach.

Parry it down with your right and return a back-handed blow with the same hand, covering your stomach with your left arm.

David strikes at Ulf's stomach with the left. Ulf parries it.

Ulf then returns a back fist (chopper) at David's face with the blocking hand.

This is a variation to show that a back fist does not have to go straight. Here Ulf angles it in to hit David behind the right jaw, just below the ear.

Master's right strikes at your stomach.

Parry it down with your left and return a back-handed blow with the same hand, covering the stomach with the right arm.

David strikes a right at Ulf's stomach. Ulf parries it down.

Ulf again returns a back fist at David's head.

Master's left strikes again at your stomach.

Parry it down with your right and return a straight blow at his face with the same hand. Entry by a pass, shifting the lead foot.

David strikes a left at Ulf's stomach. He parries it with his right.

This time Ulf counters with a straight right from the parrying position.

His right does the same.

Parry it down with your left and return a straight blow at his face with the same hand. Entry by a shuffle step, maintaining the same lead foot.

David strikes at Ulf's stomach with a straight right. Ulf parries it with his left hand.

Ulf then returns a straight left at David's face.

LESSON 5

Ripostes: 1, 2 at the Face

The Scholar strikes 1, 2, beginning with his left. Master parries with his left and ripostes with his left at your face.

Parry this riposte by catching the wrist with your left fist and striking a back-handed blow across his face with your left hand.

Ulf, in the role of the Scholar, attacks David first with a straight left. David parries.

Ulf then strikes a straight right at David, who parries it as well.

David then executes a riposte at Ulf's face. Ulf catches this with his left hand.

Ulf returns a back fist (chopper) at David's face.

Do the same with your right hand, i.e., beginning 1, 2 with your right.

This time he parries with his right and ripostes with the same. Then you catch it with your right fist and return with a back-handed blow across his face.

Ulf begins with a straight right, which David parries.

Ulf then strikes a left, which David parries as well.

Ulf catches David's right and deflects it sideways.

Ulf then strikes a chopper with his right hand at David's head.

Ripostes: 1, 2, 3 at the Face

The Scholar strikes 1, 2, 3, beginning with his left. Master parries with his right and ripostes at your stomach with his left.

Stop this with your right forearm and return with your left at his face.

Ulf throws a left at David, who parries it.

Ulf advances and throws a right at David's face, which he parries.

Ulf advances again and throws a left at David's face, which he parries.

At the final strike, David parries with the right and counters at Ulf's stomach with a straight left aimed at the mark. Ulf parries this.

Ulf then returns a straight left at David's face.

Strike 1 at the face and 2 at the stomach, beginning with your left.

This he will stop with his left and riposte 1, 2 at your face, beginning with his left. Parry with your left and return 1, 2 at his face.

Ulf strikes a left at David's face. He parries with the right hand.

Ulf advances and strikes a right at David, which he parries.

David returns with his first strike.

David returns with his second strike.

Strike 1 at the face, 2 at the face, and 3 in the stomach, beginning with your left, keeping your right fist opposite his face.

This he will stop with his right and riposte 1, 2, 3 at your stomach, which you must bar.

Ulf strikes at David's face with a straight left. David parries.

Ulf steps in with a straight right at David's face. David parries.

Ulf then steps in with a strike at David's stomach, which he parries.

David then returns the favor with a straight left, which Ulf parries.

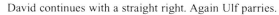

David continues with a straight right. Again Ulf parries.

David rounds off with a left at Ulf's stomach, which he parries, making sure the entire time to keep the unused fist aimed to Davi d's face and in position for a counterstrike.

Do the same with the other hand, i.e., beginning with your right.
This he will stop with his left and riposte 1, 2, 3 at your stomach, which you must bar.

The Scholar strikes with his left at the face; the Master parries with his right and ripostes with his left at the stomach.
Knock the blow down and return straight at the face. Do the same with the other hand.

LESSON 6

Scholar strikes 1, 2 at the face, beginning with the left.
Master parries and ripostes the same.

Scholar strikes 1, 2, 3 at the face, beginning with the left.
Master parries and ripostes the same.

Scholar strikes 1, 2 at the face and 3 at the stomach, beginning with the left.
Master parries and ripostes the same.

Scholar strikes 1, 2 at the face and 3 at the side, beginning with the left.
Master parries and ripostes the same.

Chapter

5

BARE-KNUCKLE CONDITIONING

Aside from hitting very hard and with accuracy, we need a few more things to round out the well-formed pugilist. Technique alone will not win the day—the truth is that strength, stamina, and wind will actually lead to victory in many real-life confrontations.

These aspects of physical fitness were deemed to be the foundation of bare knuckle, even more so than the techniques. Successful fighters had solid core body strength, both to withstand and deliver blows (as well as being able to move quickly); heart, or the ability to fight and continue to fight even when the going got tough (the bare knucklers called it "bottom"); and simple endurance to keep fighting without losing it.

ESSENTIAL ATTRIBUTES

The following is a brief description of the essential attributes of a bare-knuckle fighter. All of them deal to a great extent with psychological aspects of fighting, and several bare-knuckle teachers stress that they are absolutely essential to become a good boxer.

Wind

"Wind" refers to having a strong cardiovascular capacity. It is easy to think that because you can run for 20 miles, your capacity is at a peak. It may be, but fighting requires both the ability to sustain hard work over long periods of time as well as being able to apply 120 percent over very short periods of time again and again. So it is a common mistake to confuse the fact that you can run with the fact that you have the wind to fight. The former is a long-term, steady stress on the system; the latter involves bursts of intense effort at irregular intervals. In the good old days, matches could literally go on for hours, so being able to fight while conserving your strength also is an issue.[1]

Included in this concept is the muscular conditioning that will raise the threshold of your lactic acid endurance while fighting. Lactic acid depletion due to prolonged or intense physical activity will adversely affect your level of muscular control. Increased lactic acid endurance will give you increased endurance in general, as well as greater focus and precision.

Bottom

"Bottom" in the bare-knuckle sense does not refer to what is located on the back of your midsection; it is one part what we would call "guts" and one part an ability to withstand physical as well as mental punishment. Bottom, or the lack of it, is seen as being absolutely paramount to being able to fight well. Rephrased in modern terms, we would say that it is not possible to fight, either in self-defense or in a match, if you are too scared to act. Bottom, then, is the ability to master your fear, a fear that all thinking men will experience in a conflict. It is natural, and yet for some reason we tend to fear the fear, and that makes us lose our bottom.

Another aspect of bottom is concerned with how we react to pain. This is the second side of bottom—to take pain and keep going. This is connected to our innate ability to control fear and not be controlled by it.

The good news is that bottom can be trained to a rather high degree. You are not born with bottom; you acquire it.

Strength

All of the surviving old texts stress that strength is good; muscle mass, however, is not. The reason is simple: if you are stronger, you will be able to accelerate your strikes faster, but only to a certain level. Nature equals things out, so that as you gain muscle mass, you lose speed since greater mass needs even greater strength in order to accelerate to the same speed. That is why applying the body in the strikes is so important; it gives us the benefits f mass without the need to be so bulked up that our speed suffers.

In fact, the so-called BMI (body mass index) is a very good indicator of the ideal weight for your height, and your height determines the optimum size of your mass for your body. This is not rocket science, so you can easily deviate 5–10 kilograms (roughly 5–10 pounds) from it, but no more. (An interesting side note is that for every 5 kilograms you lose, you will gain 10 centimeters [4 inches] in your ability to jump vertically or horizontally.) The body does not care if you haul around fat or muscle; it is the weight that matters, not what it consists of. That said, greater body mass will allow you to withstand more damage and, within set parameters, allow you to strike harder, but only to a point. Then it just slows you down.

So where did we want to go with this? Bare-knuckle teachers stressed that strength is good, and they offered instruction on how to train it as best they knew, but they all cautioned against putting on weight. The history of pugilism is full of smaller fighters who destroyed much larger opponents (Dempsey versus Willard, for instance, to pick a favorite), so strength matters. Weight matters a lot less and is almost always bad if there's too much of it, no matter what it consists of.

Speed

You need to move fast if you are to be able to both land strikes and avoid them. But speed is often mistaken for what is in reality a question of accuracy and timing. Timing and speed are closely connected, and the ability to time your actions to the actions of the opponent is always more important then being fast once you move. Speed, you will find, is largely a matter of trimming waste from your movements and then timing those movements to those of your opponent. Then you will move slowly but appear fast, a paradox.

PHYSICAL CONDITIONING EXERCISES

The following exercises are aimed at conditioning the body and the delivery system, i.e., the hands and arms. The body needs to be tough enough to withstand punishment, and the hands and arms need to be tough enough to deliver it.

Conditioning the Hands

Good hands are a necessity for a pugilist, and having weak hands and wrists leads to quick defeat, regardless if it is a prizefight or a self-defense situation. In Asia, there is a longstanding tradition of conditioning the hands, and these techniques have penetrated the martial arts community in the Western world. What is not so well known is that there exists in Europe decent instructions and historical anecdotes for conditioning the hands in order to withstand hits to the harder parts of the human anatomy during a bare-knuckle fight.

Basically, conditioning the hands consists of two distinct parts. The first is increasing the strength in the muscles of the hand, wrist, and forearm. This is necessary since it is the strength of this entire delivery system and not just the hands that allows you to turn the fist and forearm into one rigid ram that will not budge no matter what it encounters. Without this strength, your hand and wrist integrity will be compromised once you hit something. This is not a case of having weak bones; it is a case of a weak delivery system.

The early 20th century heavyweight champion James Tunney was a great boxer, but he had a weak set of hands. To counter this, he set out to strengthen them. He did this by 1) doing push-ups on the fingertips, 2) squeezing a rubber ball, 3) doing single-finger push-ups against a wall, 4) striking a heavy bag, and 5) chopping trees in lumber camps during his vacations. [2] This, of course, strengthened his hands and forearms immensely— so much, in fact, that he managed to give "the Man" himself, the great Jack Dempsey, a run for his money! Everything Tunney did was aimed at increasing the integrity of his delivery system—his the hands, wrists, and arms—making sure it was strong enough to withstand the impact of repeated blows.

The second thing you must do is condition the bone structure of the hand and wrist to withstand blows. This includes thickening and strengthening the bones, fascia, tendons, and cartilage. The only way to do this is to hit things—it is that simple. The trick is to hit the right things.

Some people who work with their hands a lot—such as fishermen, carpenters, and blacksmiths—have tough hands naturally, but even they must work on conditioning them to accept an impact straight on. Remember that if you hit an opponent with, say, the force of 40 kilograms (88 pounds), your hand will receive the same amount of force back into it, and into the wrist and arm behind it. This is a Newtonian physical law, and no amount of technique will change that fact. This is why people break their hands or wrists when delivering a punch; not because they hit something hard.

To train to prevent this, you need to gradually expose your hands and wrists to stress, to such a degree that you cause minor fractures, which, when healed, result in thicker bone. This toughening by repeated impact goes for the tendons, fascia, and cartilage as well.

Tunney's method to strengthen his weak hands is interesting because it corresponds well with the recommendations given to us by earlier bare-knuckle sources. The first recommendation is to hit something that has greater density than your hand and which is heavy in itself. Enter the heavy bag. The bare-knuckle era used a different type of bag than today's solid, unyielding versions. The old bags were filled with about 22 kilograms (just under 50 pounds) of barleycorn and topped off with hay as a lid. This results in a bag with a heavy, nonyielding softness that is a lot like human flesh. Jack Dempsey recommended filling the bag with a mixture of sawdust and rags. [3] Again, it is not the rock-solid bag of today.

Modern bags are designed for use with gloves. If you hit them hard without gloves, you risk breaking something no matter how much you have conditioned your hands. The result is that you do not train the integrity of your delivery system to a great degree when hitting a heavy bag with bare knuckles. The older style of bag has a give that allows your hand to sink into the target before compacting enough to stop the blow. This not only better simulates how a body actually behaves when struck, but it also allows for excellent conditioning by offering gradually increasing resistance to the hands on impact. You can see the parallel with "iron hand" training in Asian martial arts.

Tunney also used to soak his hands in brine to make the skin thicker and leathery, giving him a harder surface, and one less prone to rupturing, across the part of the hand that impacts on the target. The idea was to create a chemical allergic reaction that dried out the hands and thereby forced the skin to thicken. (In earlier days, the Swedish army utilized the same principle by recommending to recruits with feet that blistered easily to rub them with alcohol or a solution of water and formaldehyde.) The downside is that your skin will rupture and crack, which must be countered by applying some form of moisturizing agent such as a good quality hand lotion in generous doses.

This method of conditioning is also found in iron palm training in Asia, but there is nothing magical about it. Apply a solution to the skin to thicken it, then soften the skin with some form of lotion to prevent cracking, and then hit something repeatedly to induce a solidifying of tissues through the strain of impact. It's just plain chemistry, an understanding of human anatomy, and common sense.

Conditioning the Body to Withstand Blows

It is necessary to condition the body to withstand blows. Contrary to popular belief, this has less to do with gaining the ability to absorb damage as it does with becoming familiar with the sensations of getting hit and the accompanying physical reactions (e.g., an adrenaline dump). It is, of course, possible to train the torso hard and thus increase the body's ability to withstand hits, but only to a limited extent, and it is restricted to soft tissue areas. The "iron body" tricks shown by Asian martial artists are just that—tricks.

Renowned magician Harry Houdini had a party trick to let any man hit him in the stomach as hard as he could. By practicing how to tense all the muscle in the stomach wall—not just the superficial ones (i.e., the six pack) but also the deeper ones that we usually do not have conscious control over—Houdini managed to become a hard target indeed. (The trick ultimately led to Houdini's death. One day he got hit before he could prepare properly and eventually died of internal injuries.) This is the same goal as in Asian systems—gradually the student is taught to tense all the muscle and connective tissue in the stomach wall. You can learn to do the same thing, and it will result in stronger and thicker muscle tissue, which in turn will make you more resistant to blows. Again, there is nothing magical about this, but only an understanding of human anatomy and common training sense.

How to practice, then. In Europe prior to Houdini, there seems to have been rather little emphasis on training the stomach, and aiming for the mark was considered a sure-fire way to end a fight quickly since you can't do much to increase your ability to withstand damage to the pit of the stomach. But the historical sources indicate that sparring was considered the best way to understand and acquire the ability to absorb hits and ignore the resulting pain. Toughening the body core through sparring is not the same as Houdini's method (which he borrowed from Indian yoga) or that of Asian systems, but it does accomplish something similar over a longer period of time, though to a lesser degree.

The old texts also say that sparring should be done without any protection except perhaps so-called mufflers—gloves with a bit of straw inside them. Our modern equivalent is perhaps thin mixed martial art (MMA) gloves at the very most, but preferably thinner. (I like gardening gloves without any padding or anything.) The reason seems to have been that people do get carried away while sparring, and you ought to be careful with your friend's health and he of yours. Sparring should be done using correct technique rather than fast technique so you learn not only how to hit properly but how to get hit properly. The bare-knuckle way hurts a hell of a lot more than when using thick boxing gloves, and bare-knuckle or lightly gloved sparring shows why you must be prepared for both the bodily sensations of getting hit and the mental response to those sensations.

Here are a few simple exercises that develop the ability to take a hit to the body and head. Note that it is not possible to condition the head to withstand full-force blows; you only get brain damaged if you try it, so training blows to the head should be moderate.

Exercise 1

Stand with your arms above your head, feet spread wide, preferably with no shirt to absorb impact. Have your partner strike you all over your upper body, making sure to include the sides and loins but not the groin. Do not use gloves for this exercise—bare fists only. Do a set of perhaps 50 punches, and let the person getting hit decide if it is hard enough or if it should be harder. The force should be constantly on the side of painful and unpleasant, but just barely. Gradually increase the impact until you can take five or six full blows to the body without going down. You can start by using the palms, slapping the body with gradually increased force, and then progress to fists. This training method was recommended by one of the greatest Western martial artists of all time, Benny "the Jet" Urquidez, a phenomenal fighter who could withstand immense punishment to the body. Give it a month or so and you will see a marked difference in your ability to absorb hits.

Exercise 2

Do exercise 1, but move around, using proper footwork and distancing. This exercise forces you to change how you absorb impact, since as you move a different pattern of bodily tension and relaxation is introduced. It has the added benefit of allowing your partner to practice how to move in and hit. As before, the person getting hit decides on the force of the blows. Do 50 or so and then switch roles.

Exercise 3

Start this exercise only after doing the first two exercises for at least a couple of months, unless you have prior recent experience with contact martial arts such as muay Thai or kickboxing. As you move around, your partner steps in and punches to the *front* of your stomach as hard as he can. Avoid blows to the kidneys and lower ribs, as either could cause serious damage. Only strike three or four times, and then rest and change roles. Never do this in several sets but rather do one set each as a way to feel a real hit now and then.

Exercise 4

Spar using MMA gloves and mouthguard, with the entire body as a target. Don't spar in timed rounds but rather until one of you wants a rest. Then restart and continue for 30 minutes in all. Go for the entire body, including the head, but only moderate blows to there. If you have access to full-contact masks, put them on *once* every six months and go for the head with full power while sparring, but not for more than a few hits. Getting hit in the head does not make you smarter, nor can your head be trained to absorb blows better. You just think so as the brain dies!

Strength Training

Having bodily strength is important, but you should not put on weight by joining the local gym. The reason is simple—weight will at a certain point cease to give you anything in terms of power and instead start to make you slower. Proper force in punches comes from body mechanics and speed, not weight. Even at the close of the bare-knuckle era, weight training was frowned upon since it gave mass but not durability and power. Instead, many recommended hard physical labor—such as working in mines, shifting goods in harbors, cutting trees, and blacksmithing—for acquiring the proper strength. Few people today possess this type of strength simply because fewer of us perform this sort of work.

How do we accomplish this today if we don't live on a farm or really work with our bodies daily? Well, it is a problem, but not without solution. First, avoid weights and gyms like the plague. This includes kettle bells and whatever other fitness fad comes along. Instead, focus on forms of strength training that don't require weights (manual labor, most likely) or, if that is not practical, forms that use the body as the only resistance.

In our opinion, a good place to start is a regimen that focuses on neck bridges, several kinds of push-ups and pull-ups, and squats. Some of these exercises are old, originating in India or other exotic places, and you will find them in yoga, but they were used to great effect in the 19th century by European wrestlers and boxers. They are simple and emphasize the ability to work for long intervals rather than at an extremely high resistance for short intervals, as you find in gym training. Rather than simply pressing a weight in one direction, they are dynamic and require you to have strength but also softness and a great degree of control in the movement. This makes for a much more useful form of strength training than the workout you usually get in a gym. We want muscles that are useful and allow for speed. This means limited mass and thus limited body weight.

The following exercises are just a few suggestions for developing a proper form of bodily strength. In addition, seize any chance you can to work the body by performing physical labor. It's a great way to make friends with the neighbors!

Hindu Push-Ups

This exercise is really great since it allows you to work up to high repetitions without risking the stress on joints induced by ordinary push-ups. They are also dynamic and require you to tense the entire upper body. Using the arms is simply not enough to do Hindu push-ups well.

Spread the feet and hold the hands slightly farther apart than your shoulders.

Dip your body down and as far back as possible and try to brush your chest along the floor as close to your hands as you can, then go forward.

Push up as far as possible, making sure to bend the neck and look at the ceiling. You want to create a bend in the spine by pushing your chest forward and up toward the ceiling.

Press your hands into the floor and gently press yourself back up to the starting position. Do not go back down along the floor on the return, as this carries with it a definite risk of back injury.

Bridging the Right Way

Bridging is an important exercise since it builds up the neck, which is useful for withstanding blows, but also because it builds the back and abdominal muscles to some extent. There are a lot of ways to practice the bridge; this is just one of them. *Please be careful with your neck!*

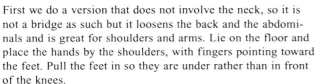

First we do a version that does not involve the neck, so it is not a bridge as such but it loosens the back and the abdominals and is great for shoulders and arms. Lie on the floor and place the hands by the shoulders, with fingers pointing toward the feet. Pull the feet in so they are under rather than in front of the knees.

Press yourself up as high as possible and, as you progress, walk the feet further in and strive to push the chest toward the hands as much as possible so that hands, shoulders, and chest are in line one above the other. Hold that position as long as possible and ease yourself down the same way you went up. Remember to bend the neck to look at the floor as you press yourself up.

Now the bridge proper. From the same starting position . . .

. . . lift your body slightly so your forehead can roll to the rear. The goal is to have the forehead and not the top of the head in contact with the floor.

When you feel established, remove the hands if it feels OK in the neck and place them on your chest. You can then try to move back and forth slightly, but remember that the neck is sensitive. A better way to add stress is to try and walk the feet further in and raise your hips as high as possible. This is both safer and harder to do, since you will be working against the strong abdominals that must both stretch and tighten to be able to cope.

Doing a Proper Squat

Squatting is great, and there are probably a million ways to do the exercise. This is an old version found in texts on wrestling from the late 19th century, such as Farmer Burns' work on physical culture. It is easy to do and very effective. Do as many as you can and repeat two or three times—unless you can pump out hundreds, that is! One important detail is that it is *much* easier to do them relatively fast since you will gain enough momentum to bounce up. *Don't!* Do this squat really slow. Going down should take about three to four seconds; take the same amount of time going up. You will feel a difference. It is better both for your strength development and your joints.

Stand erect with your hands stretched out in front of you.

As you go down, your heels should lift off the floor. Maintain your upper body in a straight position without leaning forward too much.

In the lowest position, you should have folded your legs completely. Maintain the straightness of the arms.

You can also do this exercise with the arms at your hips.

Strengthening the Wrists with the Sea Lion Push-Up

Although sea lion push-ups are perhaps not kosher in terms of antiquity, they have similarities with early wrestling exercises, so we would like to include them since they really work wonders for weak wrists. The general idea is to use the ordinary push-up to stress the wrists rather than the arms and chest by using the backs of the hands to perform the exercise and pointing the fingers in different directions!

Here you have the backs of the hands on the mat, with the fingers pointing out to the sides. In this position, you will not be able to go down very far due to the angle of the elbow, but that is of less importance. It works nonetheless.

This is as far down as it is practical to go.

And up again!

Here we have the fingers pointing inward, still with the backs of the hands on the floor.

Press yourself back into the starting position.

Maintain the tension in the body and keep facing forward as you go down.

Here we have the fingertips pointing backwards, with the backs of the hands still on the floor.

Maintain tension as you go down; face forward and do not sag.

Here is the classic push-up on the knuckles. Keep the fists more toward your waist than under your shoulders to deemphasize the stress on the upper body.

Maintain tension and face forward as you lower to the floor.

Return to the starting position.

Fingertip Push-Ups

This was one of Tunney's favorite exercises. When doing fingertip push-ups, listen to your body. If it really hurts and feels horrible, back off and rest. The most important thing to remember is that you *must* tense the entire torso package and make the body absolutely stiff as a board, with the back arching slightly upward rather than sagging down. This is also the case once you go down to the floor—keep it tense! Work your way up to as high a number as you can crank out and repeat for, say, a max of three sets.

The starting position, with eyes forward and the body stiff and slightly arched.

Go all the way down to the floor while maintaining the tension in the body and the slight arch in the lower back, facing forward as always.

Straighten the arms and push up, without sagging the back! Face forward.

Starting position for one-finger pushes against a wall. (If you are really tough like Bruce Lee, do it on the floor. The rest of us use a wall.) Maintain a slight upward arch in the finger so it does not sag downward in the joint from stress.

Lean in to the wall, maintaining the straightness of the finger and good contact with the wall. Do not let it bend.

Push yourself out, again not letting the finger bend.

CARDIOVASCULAR FITNESS THE BARE-KNUCKLE WAY

The concept of wind was very important in bare knuckle, and today's boxers also emphasize the need to be able to fight for long periods of time. The difference is that bare-knuckle matches were considerably longer than modern bouts. In spite of that, the old texts did not advocate running to get fit; instead, it was recommended that you take brisk walks several times a day. In our modern lifestyle, this might mean walking briskly to and from work, and perhaps taking a walk over lunch break.

The concept of wind was closely integrated with having a durable strength, which enabled a combatant to not run out of steam (something you see in quite a few modern full-contact matches, regardless of style). The emphasis thus was on having what we might call core strength and cardiovascular capacity to endure a long, grueling bare-knuckle contest.

To develop this level of fitness, it is essential to partake in training that emphasizes prolonged repetitions. This gives us long-lasting endurance as well as the capacity to explode into attacks. Explosiveness is based on short-term energy, but it must be backed by a long-term endurance, because without the latter the former quickly becomes useless in a fight.

Again, the preferred exercise historically was walking briskly, twice or three times a day for as much as 10 miles. You can do the same thing today, but to do it properly, do not just stroll along quietly. Instead, walk quickly and with purpose, maintaining the same pace throughout the entire walk. This is much harder than it sounds. If you live in the country, so much the better; take a walk in the countryside, but without losing the pace. Avoid the temptation to include a backpack—you don't want to add extra weight unless there are specific reasons for it, such as soldiers training while wearing their field kit. Instead, you want to work out under conditions as close to the ones you will be in during a bare-knuckle fight, which means no backpack. You will notice that your cardiovascular capacity will increase greatly. Start with 30 minutes and increase from there. As you improve, do not train longer than one hour. Instead, aim for a faster pace throughout the session. If you can keep a brisk pace for an hour, you will be fit—have no doubt about that.

SPARRING AND TRAINING THE BARE-KNUCKLE SKILLS

Sparring was considered an absolutely essential part of the path to mastery of the art. As we noted earlier, it allows you not only to increase how hard you hit but teaches you how to absorb rather hard shots to the body.

At the same time, the old texts admonish us to spar with restraint and not get carried away, to focus on good technique and keep under control at all times, regardless of what happens. If you get hit, don't get upset. Instead, consider why it happened and make sure it does not happen again. Strive to emphasize correct, relaxed techniques and movements, always maintaining control over your breathing by not panting and always breathing through the nose.

Avoid throws and the like during sparring, not because they do not work but because it is very easy to damage your training partner by accident. All throws, falls, and trips, therefore, should be practiced with care and absolute control, preferably on *budo* mats to allow for really practicing the techniques without holding back. We also recommend using so-called mufflers during sparring, which are gloves stuffed with some straw, or simply a pair of gardening gloves without any padding. Their purpose is to spare the training partner as much as possible.

NOTES

1. See *The Savage Science of Streetfighting* for some interesting commentary on the length of fights.
2. Beaumont, *The Savage Science of Streetfighting*, pp. 78–79.
3. Dempsey, *Championship Fighting*, p. 44.

Chapter

6

ADDITIONAL TECHNIQUES FROM THE EUROPEAN TRADITION

These techniques are not part of the bare-knuckle curriculum in the sense that they are described in any of the texts that have surfaced so far. But we know they existed in bare knuckle because they were specifically banned, and from those descriptions we can match them to surviving techniques in other manuals of personal combat from Europe's martial history. We have decided to include them in this book because we feel they reflect the missing elements of the bare-knuckle material, and they work very well. That was the reason why they were banned—they work a bit too well!

PUGILISTIC TECHNIQUES PRIOR TO THE BARE-KNUCKLE ERA

Striking techniques existed prior to the great English bare-knuckle era (i.e., from the 1700s to 1900). From the Middle Ages there survives a great collection of instruction on wrestling, and sprinkled among these techniques we find the strikes. (If you are interested in reading more about wrestling in the Middle Ages, I can recommend the books *Sigmund Ringeck's Knightly Arts of Combat* and *Codex Wallerstein*, both of which have a long chapters on the art of medieval wrestling.[1]) But because these strikes were grouped with wrestling techniques, it has led to the mistaken idea that no system of striking existed in earlier days. We know this to be incorrect from several sources, such as the introduction to *Flos Duellatorum* by Master Fiore dei Liberi, dated to 1409. While it does not describe any specific bare-knuckle techniques, it mentions *pugilates*—that is, people who fight with their fists. This piece of evidence, among others, lays to rest the idea that the bare-knuckle arts have a later (and predominantly English) provenance.

We also know that early unarmed combative systems encompassed boxing and other non-wrestling techniques because it can be surmised by looking at the early bare-knuckle rules, which expressly forbid such techniques as gouging the eyes, kicking the groin, throwing by the breeches, and breaking joints. The truth is that the striking parts of the earlier systems were banned in order to create something that was a bit less harmful to the participants, although a few of the techniques survived in bare knuckle, such as the cross-buttocks throw, tripping, and even a less brutal form of eye gouging (with the knuckles rather then the fingers and thumb, as it was done earlier).

Why this separation between wrestling and pugilism? The reason is probably twofold and simple. First, wrestling is more difficult to learn, especially the complex and technically advanced techniques, so in their work the masters rightly made the choice to emphasize that which was most difficult. Furthermore, wrestling was done from time immemorial mostly as a pastime and as a way of educating mind and body. That did not preclude using it in combat, nor the inclusion of brutal techniques even in its sporting form, but pugilism is another matter. It is a less forgiving activity in that it is not possible to exclude the damaging techniques since that was all the techniques there were! In other words, you cannot really fight for fun. An easy example: Jack Dempsey, known as the Manassas Mauler, was not a large man, being of average weight and height. Yet in his match with Jess Willard, a giant of a man, Dempsey broke his jaw, face bone, and ribs and knocked out some of his teeth—with gloves on.

In short, things break when you fight with the hands, and even a modicum of skill will make that certain. There are many reasons why we see so few serious injuries of that kind today, but in the historic era from Rome onward, the only "softening" ever used in pugilism consisted of hard leather straps wound over the hand!

Finally, the emphasis on wrestling during the Middle Ages may have had a social reason. Wrestling instruction from that era is found in texts that describe the curriculum of respectable schools of martial arts, texts aimed at the nobility. Pugilism may simply have been the provenience of lower social orders and thus not recorded to the same extent in the fight books of Europe. Pugilism starts to emerge in the martial arena in the late 17th and early 18th centuries, when we start to get a wider variety of reports on social events. It was, however, still socially suspect well into the 19th century, and to some degree even today it is seen as rather unrefined. So maybe that is the simple and uneventful reason for this uneven interest in wrestling and pugilism in European martial history.

We would now like to include a few of the earlier striking techniques and some other interesting moves from the treasure chest of the Western martial arts, including a short presentation on each source.

NICOLAES PETTER

In Nicolaes Petter's magnificent book on unarmed combat from 1674, there is a plate on page 55 depicting the straight strike to the face while stepping on the opponent's lead foot to prevent him from moving away.[2] This is a variation in Petter's book that does not really introduce a system of punching; rather, it is a dirty trick that presupposes that you were allowed to punch. It is therefore reasonable to surmise that striking was a technical part of combat systems prior to the 18th century.

JOHANN GEORG PASCHEN

Vollstandiges Ring-Buch, Johann Georg Paschen's book from 1659, is a favorite among martial scholars because it contains material that indicates a working system of self-defense rather than sport. It is a bit hard to follow in places due to ambiguities in the text and illustrations, but it is possible to make sense of most of the techniques if you give it some time.

The book deals primarily with freeing yourself from holds. As such it is not a wrestling book proper but a book on how to counter wrestling. It contains a few strikes and kicks as well as two parries that can be used against someone trying to strike or achieve a hold.

The elbows were used in Europe prior to the introduction of modern martial arts, and an interesting example is found in Paschen's wrestling manual. It seems to be done with the elbow traveling downward so you strike the opponent's face in a descending movement. The elbow strike to the ribs is done, by necessity of the target's location, more straight.[3]

Paschen has two more interesting striking techniques that deserve to be mentioned. The first is a strike with the stiff edge of the hand at the opponent's nose and mouth, used as a close-in technique. The second technique was to grab your opponent's hair and pull sharply backwards.

Paschen's parries are interesting because he illustrates a high and low block, which appear to be identical to the parries recommended later by the bare-knuckle masters. The high block is executed by lifting the arm to parry a strike to the face. The low block is executed by striking down and out in the manner recommend by Sullivan, for instance, to deflect a strike at the mark or sides of the ribs.

Here is a small selection of Paschen's techniques that illustrate a strike in some respect.

Strike to Chin with Hair Pull

David grabs Ulf by the hair behind the neck, pulls his head back, and strikes Ulf underneath the chin. Another option for life-or-death self-defense is to strike straight to the throat.

Ridge-Hand Strike to Face and Neck

Ulf strikes at David's nose with the ridge of the hand. This strike can be delivered from various positions and angles.

The strike can also be aimed at the opponent's throat or mouth. Here Ulf strikes David's throat.

Elbow Strikes

This elbow strike is aimed at both high and low targets. David starts with a straight strike at Ulf, who defends by deflecting as usual.

Ulf steps in and delivers a strike in the face with the elbow while maintaining control of David's arm.

David steps in with a right-hand strike, which Ulf defends with the same-side arm. Notice the change in geometry: deflection with the same-side arm creates a diagonal line, with a wide opening for Ulf to drive his elbow into David's right side.

Ulf steps in and strikes with the elbow, maintaining the control over David's arm. The strike and step must be simultaneous for the best effect. Remember not to slap him with the fleshy part of the arm but try to drive the bony part of the elbow in to his ribs.

Kicks

Kicks were not invented by savate, as proved by their existence in Paschen's text. These kicks are low and fast; in fact, you never see a leg attack that goes above the waist in the European material.

David steps in to attack with a straight strike. Ulf simply kicks low with a straight leg, aiming at the knee. This effectively stops David in his tracks, upsets his balance, and opens him up for a follow-up.

Here Ulf nails David with a low kick when both are in the guard position but still at a distance. No attack has been made; it is a way to open the engagement.

This a nice follow-up to the kick from the guard position. Ulf simply steps in with a strike to the face.

SIGMUND RINGECK

Sigmund Ringeck wrote one of the more influential texts on personal combat in the late Middle Ages. His work included sections on fighting with the long sword and with the spear (in and out of armor) as well as on unarmed combat. In his text, wrestling (or *Ringen* in German) plays an important part, and the striking attacks play a rather minor role. But striking techniques are there, and it seems as if boxers as a separate category also existed.

The more colorful striking techniques in Ringeck's book are called *Mortschlag*, or murder strikes. One of particular interest to the bare-knuckle man is aimed at the temple. This can be done most easily with a hammer fist from the front, but it also can be done from the side with a straight strike. Another interesting strike is aimed at the heart, going forward and slightly downward to create a strong strike at the heart and optimally send it into arrhythmia and cardiac arrest. This is most easily done as a follow-up technique after a block against a straight punch to the face.

We have chosen to include Ringeck's *Mortschlag* here, because they are interesting in themselves, and they complement the more modern material. These techniques are of no use in a sporting context but have a place in serious self-defense.

Hammer Strike to Heart

Ulf throws a strike at David, who blocks upward, maintaining focus and the free hand aimed at the opponent.	David then strikes at Ulf's heart from above. The idea is to allow the strike to hit and slide downward rather than striking directly inward at the target.	David then reaches up and grabs Ulf's throat, gripping the larynx with the thumb, index, and middle fingers while pushing Ulf's head back, opening him up for a strike.

Knee to Mark

David throws a straight strike at Ulf, who deflects it upward.

David then tries to follow up with either a second strike with the other hand or by reaching forward to grab Ulf. Ulf again deflects by lifting his other arm, maintaining control of David's position with the right arm.

Ulf reaches forward to take hold of David by the collar, neck, or whatever is available to grab.

Ulf then pulls David toward him and simultaneously slams his knee into the mark (the groin is too hard to hit effectively). There are, of course, many more ways to deliver a knee to the mark or another target on the lower part of the body.

Vertical Fist to Temple

Ulf throws a straight strike at David, who deflects it upwards as usual.

David then turns his fist vertical and strikes down, aiming at Ulf's temple. In a self-defense situation, this could be executed with an implement, such as keys in the hand.

NOTES

1. Lindholm & Svärd, *Sigmund Ringeck's Knightly Arts of Combat*, pp. 23–158, 173–184, 201–218. (A translation of a 15th century work, this book also has modern comments and plenty of illustrations of how the techniques are to be done.) Zabinski & Walczak, *Codex Wallerstein*.
2. Petter, *Klare Onderrichtinge der Voortreffelijcke Worstel-Konst*, p. 55, plate 1.
3. Paschen, *Vollstandiges Ring-Buch*.

Chapter

7

SELF-DEFENSE IN THE REAL WORLD

Self-defense is, for the common man and woman at least, perhaps the most misunderstood aspect of all martial arts training today. There is usually nothing wrong with the techniques and concepts presented in many martial art schools—except that you must have the skills of Bruce Lee, not to mention a lot of luck, to execute them successfully in a real self-defense situation.

Self-defense is so much more than technique. Such things as awareness and evasion are much more important than many people realize. Paladin Press has some really good books on self-defense and the handling of violence, and we recommend some in chapter 9. But first we will discuss self-defense in general and how bare knuckle fits into the picture.

Author Geoff Thompson has written several good books on self-defense based on his work as a bouncer/doorman in the less savory parts of English industrial cities, where people are hard for real, so he has some authority on the matter. In his excellent book *Watch My Back*, Thompson says that effective self-defense boils down to this: "Learn to hit fucking hard, hit first, and keep hitting until he does not move any more." This may sound harsh, but if a situation deteriorates to the point where fighting is necessary to defend yourself, it sums thing up very well.

There is, however, a misconception that self-defense is about hitting only. In reality, self-defense is 80 percent psychology, 10 percent conditioning, and 10 percent technique.

A short story from my life illustrates the importance of psychology in a confrontation. I was walking home pleasantly drunk around two in the morning, when I saw three young fellows step out onto the pavement on my side of the street up ahead. They looked at me, started talking, and looked again. This was a set-up if I ever saw one, and I knew I needed to do something or get stomped.

I walked up to the largest guy, stared into his eyes, and said, "Sorry mate, what time is it?" One of the small fish next to him said, "I'm going to kill you." I kept staring at the big guy, who was somewhat flabbergasted by my actions and the fact that I completely ignored the small guy on my right. In reality, I was observing him closely; if he made a move for me, I would have sunk my keys in his eye socket, having set them up as knuckledusters in my right-hand pocket so they protruded between my fingers. The big guy suddenly found his voice and said, "Uhm, about two." "Thank you. 'Night," I replied and walked away. They stood there for some time, and the skinny little fellow kept screaming that he was going to do me in. He did not budge an inch to put any muscle behind those words.

The point is that I took charge of the situation and commanded them instead of running or allowing them to command me. This gave me the initiative and created insecurity in their minds. (Who walks up to three guys out for a fight in the middle of the night and asks about the time?) Part of my victory was due to the psychology behind this unspoken intimidation; the second part was that I was prepared to maim them all permanently, while they were only out for a regular stomping. They wanted to beat me up old style, but no more; I would not have thought twice about sending them to the morgue.

Another point to remember is that I chose to initiate contact with these guys as a last resort. Running was not an option, and neither was a regular fight of three against one, since I was too pissed to run quickly or fight well. If I was going to have a chance, I had to deliver a really good bluff—backed up by being prepared to land the first blow and make very sure the one on the receiving end was not going to get up again. This is what real self-defense is about: less technique and more awareness, planning, and attitude.

THOUGHTS ABOUT SELF-DEFENSE

The following is a short discussion about self-defense and tactical thinking in general, collected from some of the best authorities on the subject. You can combine their knowledge with your bare-knuckle training to create a solid, complete self-defense system. If you want to go into these ideas in depth, read the works of Gavin DeBecker, Rory Miller, Geoff Thompson, and the other authors discussed in chapter 9. Just remember that, no matter from which source you get ideas and options about self-defense, what you do when it's for real always comes down to you and you alone.

The Basic Requirements of a Self-Defense System

A good self-defense system should satisfy the following criteria:

*   It should have few techniques and be easy to learn and execute.
*   It should be based on natural instincts (to avoid freezing in a sharp situation).
*   It should employ basic, sound tactics to avoid unnecessary decision-making under pressure.
*   It should work well under stress (i.e., rely mainly on gross motor skills as opposed to complex and fine skills).
*   If should fit your needs (e.g., a bar bouncer's needs will be different than those of the average office worker).
*   Perhaps the most important point, it should fit your personal disposition (i.e., it *must* fit how you are as a person).

Stress and Motor Skills

Stress is a big part of any confrontation, and it will affect you in a lot of ways. Your heart rate will increase radically when you're under the type of stress induced by a fight. (Just consider how your body reacts to something as nonviolent as speaking in public!) Generally, you will lose your fine motor skills (i.e., actions or movements that require a degree of dexterity and hand-eye coordination) at about 115 heartbeats per minute. It happens suddenly—you have fine motor control over your movements, then you just lose it. Complex motor skills (i.e., movements that require several muscle groups and a degree of cognitive thought processing to perform) are the next to go, but you can train yourself to retain them a little longer while under stress. When you lose complex motor skills, you are left with only gross motor skills, which are dependent on large muscle groups and require minimal thought to perform. Gross motor skills are not affected under stress; in fact, they almost get better. Most martial arts techniques involve gross or complex motor skills, but in many systems you often see some techniques involving fine motor skills as well. When you see techniques or systems that focus on fine motor skills, you should be suspicious of their usefulness in a live self-defense situation.

Bare-knuckle boxing usually calls on complex motor skills, with fundamental parts involving gross motor skills (e.g., tightly clenching your fists; repetitive punching). Relying entirely on gross motor skills is not necessarily a good thing. Swinging wildly, stumbling forward, and even the inability to change tactics are signs of a person relying too much on gross motor skills. To be able to adapt to a fluid situation and throw combinations, you need to operate in at least the complex range of motor skills. This makes it essential to practice under stress in order to increase your ability to maintain this level of muscular control. This amounts to not allowing the adrenaline dump and fatigue of a real fight to pump up your heart rate too much and too fast. By exposing yourself to situations during training that simulate a real fight, including such stimuli as loud noise and pain (or fear of pain), you can desensitize yourself to some degree to the real thing and thus delay the loss of the complex range of skills in a live situation.

Pain vs. Injury

Pain is a signal and an important one, but don't think you or your opponent will give up in a real fight just because of pain. Anybody can ignore pain during an altercation due to alcohol, drugs, excitement, or just will power. Many injured people, whether they've suffered broken bones or knife stabs, only notice their injuries after the fight is over. While a person is usually sensible and lucid enough to submit to a joint lock under controlled circumstances, you must be ready to actually break a limb to achieve the same thing in a real fight. There is a real difference between physical pain and structural damage, where something in the body simply cannot function anymore because it is busted, such as a broken knee.

It's important to note that we are talking about three interrelated but separate things here—violence, pain, and injury. They are not identical but should be seen as steps on a ladder, where the latter usually includes the former but not the opposite. If you induce mechanical damage, you will cause pain through violence, but you can do violence to someone without really inducing pain or mechanical damage. See the difference? Consider the drug addict who does not feel pain, yet if you fracture his skull he will fall unconscious, or if you break his arm, he can't make use of it even though he does not feel pain. The conclusion is that in self-defense, mechanical damage is the sure way to go, but it is also the most extreme path and the most difficult to justify legally, whereas violence or physical pain is more moderate as long as no real damage is done.

Avoidance and Reading the Situation

If you avoid situations and places where you know trouble exists, you will save yourself a great deal of hassle. It is better to be able to recognize when a fight is in the making and leave the scene before it erupts instead of battering the other guy with fists or a beer glass. Know when and where it is safe to walk rather than having to pull a knife to fend off an aggressive street person. In short, knowledge of where trouble might occur and how to avoid it without violence is often worth a lot more than technique and weapons.

While it is possible to be physically attacked without warning, usually there are early indications of where things are going. You need to know how to see the trouble ahead and change your route. For example, you might recognize an aggressor "interviewing" you to see if you are safe to attack. By avoiding, defusing, or walking away from the arising situation, you save yourself a lot of problems. If he starts to psyche himself up by raising his voice and growling, try to stay calm and talk him down instead of allowing him to spiral up his aggression, as he intends. You could simply take him out at once without further ado, but talking people down works much more often than you might think. The loud mouth is just out to prove something, so let him. You are bigger than that; admit that he is the boss and leave. That is usually it. If, on the other hand, you have people there who are dependant on you, things change. If your wife or child is present and he is presenting a potential threat to them, give him one chance to leave and then do what you have to if no other way seems forthcoming.

Basically, you want to make yourself a hard target. Being a hard target does not mean being the baddest ass on the block, but one who can smell a fight five minutes before it starts and take whatever measures to emerge on the winning side, regardless of what that entails.

Have a Game Plan

Instead of having an "it can't happen to me" attitude, form a game plan for various ugly situations. By doing scenario training with friends (covered in the next chapter), you will get a feeling of what can happen and how fast it can happen. Be prepared to be surprised, even if you are aware of your surroundings. You will probably feel fear and physically weak. Shaking legs, trembling voice, and going white (the blood leaving the skin) are all natural products of adrenal release. Some of these signs can be covered, while others are harder. Try getting into the cold, rational mindset of the hunter. Be prepared to use your body so you don't freeze up. You may want to use some physical techniques to counter the effects of adrenal rush. For example, look from side to side to avoid tunnel vision. This is important so you don't miss any partners the aggressor may have.

Also have a game plan for the aftermath of a violent encounter. If you don't have a real reason to stay, disappear from the place.

Use the Fence Strategy

It is now getting close and personal. If you sense that this is going down, you should put up your "fence." You need to put your hands (or lead hand) in the important space between you and the aggressor. It is the same concept as the bare-knuckle boxers keeping their hands out in front of them, except your hands are not clenched into fists. The best way to do this is to train yourself to let your open hands "talk" to the other person so it seems natural and nonaggressive. It should seem comfortable and be done without thought. Try not to touch the aggressor, as this can trigger a physical attack. Don't let the aggressor come so close that he can touch you either. If you feel bad vibes, don't shake the aggressor's hand. It is better to be impolite then bruised. If he insists on trying to shake your hand or touch your fence hands, put him down at once. Geoff Thompson's books contain really good, in-depth material on this.

The Preemptive Strike

When the shit hits the fan, one option is the preemptive strike. You've assessed the situation and realize your best chance to defend yourself is by hitting first, then hitting hard as many times as necessary to end it. Target the jaw or head to finish the fight. If the situation is particularly dangerous, such as an attempted mugging, run after the initial strike, as it buys you time to escape. If you are up against a determined aggressor and stay to try and finish him off, it may only give him time to recover and destroy you.

The preemptive strike solution is advocated because it is effective, and it agrees with the basic tenets of bare-knuckle fighting. Your weapons—your hands, elbows, and head—are usually close to the aggressor's head. If you launch an unexpected, sudden attack, the first strike will usually hit its target with power. But the preemptive response is usually more difficult to justify legally, so don't hang around afterward.

Self-Defense and the Law

You should understand the law and claim self-defense in the correct manner when giving your statement to the police. Many people who successfully defended themselves have been convicted for what they said afterward and not for what was really done by either party. Post-assault stress, which you may suffer from, can include time and memory distortion and loss (so called tachypsychia). You may also feel an urge to talk about the incident, if only to redeem yourself. All this affects your ability to give an objective statement to the police. If you end up in court months later, what you said back then will be used, and to the letter.

So make sure you know your rights, and don't get stressed/psyched out by the police. If you are not totally clear-minded, ask to wait to make a statement until the next day or until you see a lawyer. You probably feared for your life, and you did what you did because it felt absolutely necessary.

Training: You Get Out What You Put In

If you train in tag sparring only, you are probably going to perform the same way in reality. Therefore you want to learn to always hit as hard as possible, with as close to zero telegraphing as possible, and as often as needed to put an end to the threat.

If you are not naturally tough, you can train that part up as well. Compliance or submissive behavior during training can make you react in the same manner in real life. Don't stop when the training session or a real fight goes bad, you are hurt, or whatever—never give up!

When you are satisfied with your physical and psychological development, you must work to maintain it. You want to be able to switch the "go" button on and off, meaning you should be able to attack instantly without having to go through the entire escalating ritual of violence that nontrained people perform. Instead, train to go from calm as the pope at prayer to violent aggression in the blink of an eye.

When you start training with aggression and adrenaline, it will soon become easy to turn on the rush and energy, but it not equally easy to suddenly turn it off. This requires more training and good partners. To learn to stop, you and your training partner should have a secret stop word. You should not stop defending yourself in training until your partner says the word stop. *Don't use a word that you can expect to hear in a real confrontation.* You don't want to pull back from defending yourself before the aggressor has been completely subdued just because he inadvertently blurted out the word.

Usually, we train for fun and recreation. People are relaxed and friendly. This is not the case during a typical assault on the street. Do some training scenarios where the attacker goes in full throttle, and have the exercise leader stop the session only when you call the stop word if you've been overcome or when you are going from self-defense to battering the attacker. The exercise stops instantly when the word is used by anyone.

BARE-KNUCKLE BOXING AS A SELF-DEFENSE SYSTEM

Bare knuckle works well as a self-defense method. It contains strikes, throws, and a few basic kicks, so it is simple to learn. The techniques are powerful, which means you get a good payoff for each shot you land. It relies on gross and some complex motor skills, which gives you an edge in a sharp situation since you can usually expect to lose all fine motor skills during an altercation. It works regardless of which clothes you wear, what surface you will be on, the space you will fight in, or how many attackers you meet. Bare knuckle is also easy to practice alone or with friends, because you need very little to train and enjoy its benefits.

In order to be able to use this art as meaningful form of self-defense, a few points have to be considered:

- You must be able to do the basic punches and blocks.
- You must have hands that are up to the task, which means undergoing some form of conditioning.
- You must be willing to hit the other person.

The basic prerequisite is that you must have the physical ability to strike blows and to take blows. Secondly, you must be able to withstand the psychological pressure of a bare-knuckle fight, what was called having "bottom" during the classic bare-knuckle era. And then it is a question of application, of why and when to apply your bare-knuckle skills in a real confrontation. After you've learned the fundamental techniques and tactics of this age-old fighting method, you need to adapt it to your own requirements for real-world self-defense.

The Mentality of Bare Knuckle in Self-Defense

As a self-defense system, bare knuckle is a straightforward. The goal is to hit your opponent first and continue hitting until it is all over. If there is more than one opponent, then it is even more important to not be tied up in a one-on-one wrestling match but to be able to move around and use the hands to control (read attack) the attackers. If you are caught by surprise and *get* hit first, bare-knuckle training gives you the bottom to get back into the fight.

To hit first and hit till it is all over. This mentality of bare knuckle serves well for a real self-defense situation, which often is a sudden, fast-paced, close-up fistfight. But you must be able stop when you've won and it is over. Many people who are not used to the adrenaline cocktail continue pounding their assailant until it goes from a self-defense situation to a brutal assault or even homicide of the downed opponent. It has happened. Even if it doesn't go that far, the result of a few good strikes can be bleeding, damaged teeth, and broken bones. It does not look good for the police or bystanders if you are still looking good while your opponent looks like he's been through the meat grinder.

Professional Needs

If your work environment includes violence, you have to consider whether bare knuckle is your best choice for personal training. Bare knuckle suits many, but perhaps not all, professional applications. While it works well for strict self-defense situations, it is not equally appropriate for apprehension and detention work. If your work involves controlling aggressive people (e.g., felons as a guard, or patients as a caretaker), in all probability bare knuckle would be unsuitable for your specific needs, since it rather quickly escalates into mechanical damage when applied correctly.

If you need to use open hands in your work (e.g., for shooting), then an open-hand system may suit you better. For police work, we recommend ESDS (Explosive Self Defence System) created by Swedish police officer Slavo Gozdzik under the auspices of the International Police Defensive Tactics Association (IPDTA). There are many other good systems out there, but ESDS is one of the best we've seen for the professional in our more than 25 years of experience with martial arts, military arts, and self-defense.

For military hand-to-hand combat, the object is other than self-defense and therefore outside this discussion, but we like the Fairbairn-Applegate line of military combatives as taught, for instance, by Matt Temkin. It most be understood, however, that there are differences between military hand-to-hand combat and military fitness and toughness training. When you train for fitness, you can choose whatever system you like, which is what many military units do. There is, of course, a long history of boxing and pugilism training in the military (see, for example, the manual *Boxing* from the United States Navel Institute, available from Paladin Press).

Chapter

8

SCENARIO-BASED BARE-KNUCKLE TRAINING

Scenario training is a very useful form of training, practiced nowadays by virtually everyone who uses or who may face violence in their daily jobs, as well as by individuals who want to amp up the intensity of their self-defense training. The core idea is to train under circumstances that reflect as close as possible the actual situations where you may have to use your training. That means *not* in the dojo or in typical workout clothes! Instead, practice in your everyday clothing, including shoes and jackets, or run some scenarios outside in the rain at night. Stand or walk about as you do outside, with hands in pockets, and have someone try to knock you down, and then try to defend yourself. The scenarios are limited only by your imagination, but we present some scenario-based training methods here to get you started. Remember, you will only get as good as your partner gives it, so make it intense and as real as possible.

TRAINING METHOD 1: RECOVER FROM COVER UP

The designated attacker starts to wildly throw punches at you, and you start with the natural reaction to cover up to protect yourself. You have to try to get back into the game. It is not that easy, and many trained martial artists have a hard time getting their techniques to work. You can start this off more gently by having the aggressor come at you with open-hand (i.e., palm) strikes as you cover up, then escalate to more aggressive attacks.

TRAINING METHOD 2: ATTACKED FROM BEHIND

The aggressor hits you from behind in the small of the back, hard enough to cause pain and a natural response but without injuring you. You have to recover from whatever position you end up in and start fighting.

TRAINING METHOD 3: GETTING OFF THE GROUND

An attack from behind hits you in the back of the head, and you go down to the floor. You need to get off the ground while defending yourself from further attack. Here are some ideas for getting up:

- Hit him hard on the thighs to get him to back away. Do this especially when he is towering above you and hitting down on you.
- Use your arms as hooks to climb up his body. Works well if you are dizzy or there are multiple aggressors trying to pound you. You may get a chance to throw him down as you grapple up his body.
- Slam your head into his stomach or chest, driving forward as you get up. A good option if you are seated as well.
- If you cannot get up, do you have a plan?

TRAINING METHOD 4: PREEMPTIVE STRIKE

The aggressor is interviewing you, and you see where it is leading. You decide to take the chance and fire the first shot. Of course, you want a clean knockout with the first punch. How do you set this up to get the best result? This training method can be set up in an infinite numbers of scenarios:

- In a doorway. Can you get a chance to close the door and be safe after hitting him? Try with two or more aggressors as well.
- In a bar. Can you safely leave the place if you put him down? Try with two or more aggressors as well. Even if you can take out one person, what then?
- On an unlit street or under a lamppost with bad lighting. Do you see the aggressor's hand or not? Does he have a knife in the hand?

TRAINING METHOD 5: HIDDEN KNIFE

The aggressor tells you everything is cool and turns partly away while putting his hand in his pocket. Is he reaching for a knife? The situation tells you that it is going bad. Take him out before he can use the weapon. This is a preemptive attack. *Do not wait for him to remove his hand from his pocket.* He has a knife, so take him out!

TRAINING METHOD 6: CREATING DISTANCE

You are already close to the aggressor and he gets closer. You shove him away hard and then step back and create even more distance between you. If you stay close, his natural reaction may be to fight, but by creating a greater distance, he may actually get a flight response and leave. Practice this with your verbal de-escalation skills.

TRAINING METHOD 7: DISORIENTATION

You will start with the forehead on a partner's back while he is positioned on the ground on all fours. Then, with the head in the same spot, start to run around him as fast as you can. Usually about one minute will suffice. Then try to remain steady and fight the aggressor or aggressors that wait for you. The dizziness you feel simulates adrenaline stress you would be under in a real fight, coupled with the feeling you might have if you got hit hard. When it is hard to stand up, it is not that easy to fight. Try it out and learn from the experience!

TRAINING METHOD 8: SUDDENLY SURROUNDED

One aggressor is interviewing you when one or more companions come up from the side or behind. Try out different responses here. What do you say to the aggressors? How can you position yourself when there are two? When there are three?

TRAINING METHOD 9: TWO ON ONE

With two aggressors, one grabs hold of you and the other tries to punch you out. You have to fend off both of them.

TRAINING METHOD 10: BREAK FOR THE DOOR

You're indoors, and two aggressors are interviewing you. You want to go for the door. How to get by these two opponents? Do you have anything to throw at them? Do you have the opportunity to really punch them?

TRAINING METHOD 11: GROUP POUNDING

You are under attack by a small group, say about four or five people. You will need to be mobile and extremely aggressive to survive.

TRAINING METHOD 12: GROUP SQUEEZE

You are attacked by at least four people with big training mitts, who try to squeeze you totally flat. You are allowed to hit the mitts as hard and much as you can. If you can't keep moving, then they will flatten you out.

TRAINING METHOD 13: THE GAUNTLET

You will pass between two lines of people, all wearing big training mitts and ready to slam you as you pass. You will have to push through the line while continuously punching away.

TRAINING METHOD 14: FIGHT BYSTANDER

Two small groups are fighting, and you need to protect your space without getting hurt or involved. Figure out how to cover up, preferably doing your protective part without even showing it so nobody mistakes you for a combatant.

TRAINING METHOD 15: FENCING WITH THE HANDS

Learn how to speak with your hands and use your fence and body positioning without it becoming obvious to others. At first, practice at home in front of the mirror. When you start to feel OK with it, test it out with a knowing friend. When you think it looks normal, try it out on unknowing friends. If they don't find it manufactured or strange, you have come a long way with your "speaking hands."

Chapter
9

RECOMMENDED SELF-DEFENSE BOOKS

Here are some recommendations for further reading if you want to learn more about self-defense and the nature of violence. All these authors and their books deal in an insightful way with a topic that does not really lend itself to writing.

Ned Beaumont's first book, *Championship Streetfighting*, is about boxing as a martial art, with interesting reflections from fighters of old. As you may have already figured out, the book's title pays homage to one of the greatest boxing (and bare-knuckle) books of all time, *Championship Fighting* by Jack Dempsey. It focuses on American boxing, with hints of the bare-knuckle era (from about 1869 onward). We may not share his belief that boxing evolved from bare knuckle over the last hundred years after remaining almost the same for about 1,000 years, but we wholeheartedly agree that rules and gloves made all the difference in the evolution of the modern sport of boxing from its pugilistic roots. Beaumont has it mostly right when he speaks about boxing and its body mechanics, although his disparagement of other martial arts is one of the major negatives of the book. We see *Championship Streetfighting* more as an interesting reflection on the history and development of American boxing than a book about self-defense, but if you are interested in bare knuckle and boxing, we recommend it.

The Savage Science of Streetfighting is the follow-up to Beaumont's *Champion Streetfighting*. It is less concerned with the basics and techniques and more with training. It focuses mostly on the sport of boxing, although it provides some perspective on bare knuckle as well. We like the section on physical training best, with its solid advice on good-old road work and other classic training methods. We also like the part on weight training, which is remarkably close in many parts to what we used ourselves and recommended for our students. We recommend you start with Beaumont's first book, but read this one too if want to know more about sound physical training from a boxing perspective.

Gavin DeBecker's *The Gift of Fear* is very well written and one of the best books on this subject. Enough said— get the book and read it. What we tend to fear is the feeling of fear rather than the thing that brought it on. Fear is, in essence, a chemical reaction in the body. This book helps you understand what it is, how it works, and why it is good for you. You can even make fear an ally in a fight.

Mark "Animal" MacYoung has written many books about self-defense. The following are some recommendations, but if you like the information he presents, you can continue to explore his work. His style of writing might put some people off, but remember that it is the information you want, and his information is good.

Cheap Shots, Ambushes, and Other Lessons (His first book.)

A Professional's Guide to Ending Violence Quickly (Maybe the best of his books.)

Violence, Blunders, and Fractured Jaws
Fists, Wits, and Wicked Right
Knives, Knife Fighting, and Related Hassles (While there are many books out there about knives and knife fighting, there are not that many good ones about the reality of it.)

Don Pentecost wrote about real-world knife fighting in the small but informative book called *Put 'Em Down, Take 'Em Out!* This is probably the best book on knife fighting ever published, helping you understand how knife attacks really occur and what you can and should do to survive one (such as forget the fanciful systems). Find a copy of this out-of-print booklet and learn from it.

Geoff Thompson has written many books about self-defense, but we recommend starting with *Dead or Alive* or his autobiographic *Watch My Back*. In *Dead or Alive*, he gives his opinions of such bad guys as fight seekers, muggers, rapists, and serial killers. Prevention, including situational awareness and target hardening, is presented and discussed. It is not a pleasant read, but crucial if you really are interested self-protection. In the second book, he tells about his experience as a bouncer, and his takes on violence and self-defense are interesting. (Among other things, he argues for the "hit first" option, which he used in his line of work.)

Peyton Quinn's first book was the classic *A Bouncers Guide to Barroom Brawling*. In it, Quinn describes such things as why fights occur, the psychology of the bully, how bullies select their victims, the concepts of "interviewing" and "woofing," and much more. After emphasizing the importance of awareness and avoidance as the best solution for possibly violent situations, he goes on to present technical solutions and training.

Real Fighting is about adrenal stress conditioning through scenario-based training. We agree wholeheartedly with this training concept. Besides presenting a lot of useful information about scenario-based training, Quinn discusses the proper mindset for self-defense, which is a relaxed mind. Easy to say, but harder too achieve, so put some time in to understand the concept and then practice it through scenario-based training.

These are both really good books about violence and fighting (even if we consider *Real Fighting* to be the better of the two) and are well worth including in your self-defense library.

Rory A. Miller may not have published any books on self-defense yet, but you can find some of his valuable articles on the Internet. Look for "The Four Basic Truths of Violent Assault" and "A Strategy and Tactics Primer for the Martial Artist."

BIBLIOGRAPHY

The following list is not complete in any way, but it consists of the works we made use of that are readily available, including those in library collections. Most of the modern editions are still available from the publishers.

Allanson-Winn, R.G. *Boxing*. London: A.D. Innes & Co., 1897.

Art & Practice of English Boxing. London: W. Gliden, 1807.

Barry, Edward Rev. *A Letter on the Practice of Boxing*. London: A. Grant, 1789.

Beaumont, Ned. *Championship Streetfighting*. Boulder, CO: Paladin Press, 1997.

————. *The Savage Science of Streetfighting*. Boulder, CO: Paladin Press, 2001.

Boardman, John. *The History of Greek Vases*. London: Thames & Hudson, 2001.

Boxing Made Easy: or the Complete Manual of Self Defence. New York: Dick & Fitzgerald, date unknown.

Brown, Terry. *English Martial Arts*. Norfolk: Anglo-Saxon Books, 2002, 2006.

Burns, Martin. *Lessons in Wrestling and Physical Culture*. Correspondence course, 1912.

Cod.HS.3227.a. *Döbringers fechtbuch*.

DeBecker, Gavin. *The Gift of Fear*. New York: Dell Publishing Co., 1997.

Dempsey, Jack. *Championship Fighting*. New York: Prentice Hall, 1950.

Doumas, Christos. *Santorini: A Guide to the Island and Its Archaeological Treasures*. Athens: Ekdotike Athenon, 1995.

Fewtrell, Thomas. *Boxing Reviewed, or the Science of Manual Defence*. London: Scatcherd & Whitaker et al, 1790.

Godfrey, John. *Treatise Upon the Useful Science of Defense*. London: T. Gardner, 1747.

Golding, Louis. *The Bare-Knuckle Breed*. New York: A.S. Barnes & Co., 1954.

Gorman, B. & P. Walsh. *King of the Gypsies*. Lytham, 2002.

Hand, Stephen. *English Swordsmanship*. Highland Village, TX: Chivalry Bookshelf, 2006.

Homer. *The Illiad*.

Lee, W.F. *The Art of Boxing and Self Defence*. Newspaper series, reprinted in *The Classical Pugilism and Bare-Knuckle Boxing Companion, Vol. 2*, by Jake Shannon.

Lindholm, David & Peter Svärd. *Sigmund Ringeck's Knightly Arts of Combat*. Boulder, CO: Paladin Press, 2006.

———. *Sigmund Ringeck's Knightly Art of the Longsword*. Boulder, CO: Paladin Press, 2003.

MacYoung, Mark. *A Professional's Guide to Ending Violence Quickly*. Boulder, CO: Paladin Press, 1996.

McGovern, Terry, James Corbett, et al. *How to Box*. Boulder, CO: Paladin Press, 2005 (reprint).

Mendoza, Daniel. *The Art of Boxing*. Dublin: M. O'Leary, 1792.

Modern Manhood. London: unknown publisher and publication date.

Paschen, Johann Georg. *Vollstandiges Ring-Buch*, 1659.

Pedly, John. *Greek Art and Archaeology*. London: Laurence King, 1998.

Pentecost, Don. *Put 'Em Down, Take 'Em Out!* Boulder, CO: Paladin Press, 1988.

Petter, Nicholaes. *Klare Onderrichtinge der Voortreffelijcke Worstel-Konst*. 1674.

Plato. *Gorgias*.

———. *Protagoras*.

Price, Edmund. *The Science of Self Defence*. New York: Dick & Fitzgerald, 1867.

Quinn, Peyton. *A Bouncer's Guide to Barroom Brawling*. Boulder, CO: Paladin Press, 1990.

———. *Real Fighting*. Boulder, CO: Paladin Press, 1996.

Shannon, Jake (ed). *The Classical Pugilism and Bare-Knuckle Boxing Companion, Volumes 1 and 2*. Lulu.com, 2005.

Sullivan, J.E. *Boxing: A Manual Devoted to the Art of Self Defence*. New York: American Sports Publishing Co., 1893.

Swift, Owen. *Boxing Without a Master*. William Berry & Co., New York, 1851.

The Complete Art of Boxing. London: Follingsby, 1788.

Thompson, Geoff. *Dead or Alive*. Chichester: Summersdale, 2004.

———. *Watch My Back*. Chichester: Summersdale, 1994.

U.S. Marine Corps. *Combat Conditioning: The Classic U.S. Marine Corps Physical Training and Hand-to-Hand Combat Course*. Boulder, CO: Paladin Press, 2001.

United States Naval Institute. *Boxing* (1943, revised 1950). Boulder, CO: Paladin Press, 2006 (reprint).

Zabinski, Grzegorz and Bartlomiej Walczak. *Codex Wallerstein: A Medieval Fighting Book from the Fifteenth Century on the Longsword, Falchion, Dagger, and Wrestling*. Boulder, CO: Paladin Press, 2002.